THE GOSPEL OF JOHN

◄ ◄ ◄ ◄ ◄ + ► ► ► ► ►

SPECIAL **ALPHA COURSE** EDITION

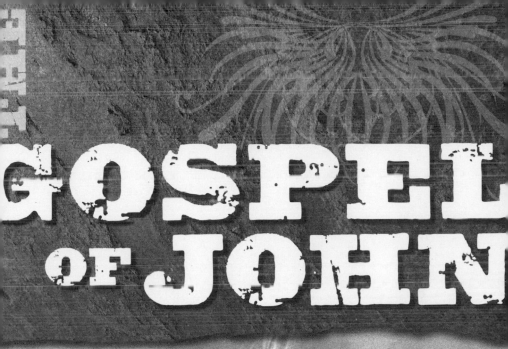

GOSPEL OF JOHN

SPECIAL **ALPHA COURSE** EDITION

Alpha

Alpha Resources
Alpha North America

TABLE OF CONTENTS

NOTES ABOUT THE IMPORTANCE OF GOD'S WORD

LIFE STORIES

WHAT IS THE ALPHA COURSE?

THE ALPHA COURSE is a fifteen-session practical introduction to the Christian faith designed primarily for non-churchgoers and new Christians. It is an opportunity for people of all backgrounds to explore the meaning of life in a safe, fun, and non-threatening atmosphere.

MORE THAN 8 million people have completed the Alpha course since it started more than twenty-five years ago at Holy Trinity Brompton church in London, England. Today the course is being run worldwide—meeting in homes, churches, universities, military posts, prisons, and workplaces, and is supported by churches of every different and major denomination.

DURING THE WEEKLY sessions, Alpha guests share meals, listen to a series of talks, and then have small group discussions. Each talk covers a fundamental question, such as: "Who is Jesus?" "Why Did Jesus Die?" "Why and How Do I Pray?" and "Does God Heal Today?"

EVERYONE IS WELCOME to attend. People come from many different backgrounds and hold many different viewpoints, but most come with the same basic objective: to establish whether God and Jesus Christ have any real relevance for their lives.

WE HOPE THAT this special edition of the Gospel of John will be valuable to anyone seeking to learn about Jesus.

WHY AND HOW SHOULD I READ THE BIBLE?

Text excerpted and adapted from the Alpha course talk by Nicky Gumbel: "Why and How Should I Read the Bible?" For the full talk, attend an Alpha course near you (see page 57) or refer to the book Alpha—Questions of Life, *by Nicky Gumbel.*

THE BIBLE IS the most popular book in the world. It has been translated into well over two thousand languages—that's over ten times more than any other book ever written. It's the world's bestseller by several miles. Forty-four million copies of the Bible are sold every year.

The Bible is also the most powerful book in the world. One former British Prime Minister described it as "high explosive" because it has the power to change lives. My own life was changed, radically, through reading this book. But why? Why is it so popular? Why is it so powerful? The answer is that the Bible is the way God communicates with us.

◀ The Bible: The Manual for Life ▶

THE BIBLE IS, first of all, a manual for life. God has spoken. He has revealed Himself. The whole of the Bible is God-breathed—it's inspired by God. Of course, He didn't dictate it; He used human authors. Over fifteen hundred years, at least forty authors—kings, scholars, philosophers, fishermen, poets, statesmen, historians, doctors—wrote different types of literature such as history, poetry, prophecy, and letters. The claim of this book is that it is 100 percent the work of human beings, but it is also 100 percent inspired by God.

"How can this be? How can I know the Bible is true?"

HERE IS AN analogy: Sir Christopher Wren, perhaps the greatest English architect of his time, built St. Paul's Cathedral. He started building it in 1676 and it took him thirty-five years. Sir Christopher Wren "built" St. Paul's Cathedral, but he didn't lay a single stone. Other people did that. But he directed the whole operation, he inspired it, he was the architect behind it. In the same way, God Himself didn't "write" this book; He used human authors. But He inspired them, He was the architect behind it, He brought it about. Every stone in St. Paul's Cathedral is there because Sir Christopher Wren intended it to be there. And the Bible is, we believe, as God intends it to be.

Because the Bible is inspired by God, it can be our supreme authority. It's our authority for what we believe, what we base our faith on, and how we act. Through it we find out what is right in God's eyes and what is wrong in God's eyes. We discover God's views about work, pressure, singleness, marriage, raising children, giving, forgiving. It's full of practical material on how to live life as a believer in Jesus.

"But the Bible is just a bunch of rules. It sounds so restrictive! If I follow this, it's going to ruin my life! It's going to spoil all the things that are fun."

DOES A RULEBOOK, a manual for life, take away our freedom, or does it give us freedom?

A few years ago when my son was eight years old, he was a very keen football (soccer) player. One day his coach set up a special match: twenty-two eight-year-old boys playing, with all the parents invited. So we went along. I arrived there only to find that there were twenty-two boys and no coach. The coach was going to serve as referee and he had gotten the time wrong.

A referee was needed and I was chosen. Now, I had a bit of a problem: The field had not been marked off so there were no boundaries, and all these little boys had arrived wearing exactly the same thing. I wasn't prepared to be the referee—I hadn't come with a whistle, I didn't know the names of the boys, and I didn't know the rules! I mean, I knew *some* of the rules, but not enough to call a proper foul, and the rules keep changing in football, don't they?

As the game went on, it descended into more and more chaos. Eventually there were about four boys lying injured on the field. It just looked like a battlefield out there! When the coach finally arrived, marked the field, and took over, the boys had a great game. He could impose the rules, call the fouls, and keep the play moving.

The question is this: Were those boys more free when I was refereeing, or were they more free when someone was in control, someone was enforcing the rules? They had a much better time once the referee arrived because they had freedom within guidelines, and everyone knew where the boundaries were.

God loves us. He hasn't given us this manual to *restrict* our freedom; He has given it to us to set us free to enjoy life as He intended us to live it.

◀ The Bible: God Speaks ▶

THE BIBLE IS God speaking to us. It's a love letter from God.

Just before my wife and I got engaged, I went away for three and a half weeks. During that time, we wrote to each other every day. Each morning I looked for a letter from her and when I saw one I felt this excitement, this thrill. Why? The letter in itself wasn't what it was about; it was because of the relationship—it was a letter from the person I love. And I wanted to know what she was saying.

If you look up John, chapter 5, verses 39 and 40 (on page 13), you'll see these words of Jesus, "You diligently study the Scriptures because you think that by them you possess eternal life. These are the Scriptures that testify about me, yet you refuse to come to me to have life." Jesus is saying that the Bible itself is not *it*. The Bible is so wonderful and exciting only because it's about Jesus. It's a love letter from God. It helps us to come into a relationship with God through Jesus Christ.

Some people have really studied the Bible, they've underlined it, they've studied commentaries on the Bible, they've learned Greek and Hebrew so that they can study the Bible in its original languages. But if they don't have a personal relationship with Jesus Christ, they are missing the point. If *all* we do is try to read the Bible without that relationship, we're missing the whole point. God still speaks to us today through the Bible.

"How can that be? How does God speak? I'm just reading words written long ago. How can they possibly mean anything to me?"

MARTIN LUTHER SAID this: "The Bible is alive. It speaks to me. It has feet, it runs after me. It has hands, it lays hold of me." What happens when God speaks? Well, first of all, He brings faith to people who are not Christians.

Sometimes people say, "Well, I don't have any faith. How can I be a Christian?" The apostle Paul in one of his New Testament letters says that faith comes by hearing, and hearing comes by the word of God. Many people read or hear the Bible and come to faith in Jesus Christ.

When we have that personal relationship with Jesus, the Bible speaks to us. As we study it, we find words that help us with our daily lives. It never ceases to amaze me that this book is about a person who lived two thousand years ago with whom we can actually have a personal relationship. We can speak to Him and He speaks to us through this book.

Communication is vital to any relationship. That's how we develop relationships; that's how relationships grow and strengthen. It's like with a child: When a baby is born, it needs food, regular food, to grow. It's no good saying, "Oh, that's so exciting, we've got a new baby!" and then just putting it out in the garden and ignoring it. If you want the baby to grow, you have to feed the baby. If you come to faith in Christ and you want to grow in your faith, you have to feed your faith. Jesus says His Word is spiritual food; His Word helps us to grow. It brings joy and peace when we're going through difficult times. It gives us wisdom, it challenges us, it guides us.

"So how do I get started? The Bible is an awfully big book . . ."

TIME IS THE first thing. Time is our most valuable possession. If you want to grow as a Christian, you need to set aside time to read the Bible. I wouldn't suggest setting aside a very long time to begin with—maybe start with about seven minutes each day. Choose the part of the day that you think you're at your best. For some it's early morning, for some it's late at night, or it might be lunchtime. But I would suggest, rather like with food—little and often.

Place is the second important factor. I would suggest that you find somewhere that's quiet, where you're on your own. I have a place where I know I'll be absolutely quiet—I go with a cup of coffee, a diary to write down distracting thoughts, and a notebook to write down if I sense God is saying something and to write down my prayers.

Method is the third factor. Ask God to speak to you. Read the passage, maybe ten or twelve verses, and ask yourself: "What does it say? What does it mean? How does it apply to my life?" Take notes in your notebook and then respond to what you sense God is saying to you by praying and going into your day putting what you've learned into practice.

I think you'll find that if you do this on a regular basis, over the years, day by day, God speaks to you—sometimes in very ordinary ways, and sometimes in very important ways.

Father, I thank You for the word of God. Thank You that You speak through the Bible. And Lord, that's my prayer: that You would speak to me as I read this book. Help me to listen for Your voice. In Jesus' name, Amen.

HOW DOES THE GOSPEL OF JOHN FIT INTO THE BIBLE?

THE BIBLE, GOD'S Word to us, is made up of sixty-six books and is divided into two main sections—the Old Testament and the New Testament. The Old Testament was written and took place before Jesus' life on earth, while the New Testament was written after His death and resurrection. John's Gospel is found in the New Testament and is one of the accounts of Jesus' life and ministry.

The Old Testament

THE OLD TESTAMENT describes the beginnings of the world and how the first human beings rebelled against God and introduced sin into creation. (Sin in Greek means to "miss the mark" and describes a separation or turning away from God.) The Old Testament points toward God's ultimate plan for our salvation (deliverance from sin and the penalties of sin). That plan was to send His Son into the world to take the punishment for all human sin and to reestablish an eternal connection to Him.

The Old Testament gives the history of the Hebrew people (the Jews) who descended from Abraham, a man who loved, trusted, and served God many thousands of years ago (Jesus was born from Abraham's bloodline). The Old Testament also includes prophecies about the future, as well as songs and poetry that reveal the depth of the Hebrew people's love for and worship of God. You may be familiar with some of the psalms (poetry), proverbs (wise sayings), and accounts that are found in the Old Testament, such as Noah's ark, the exodus from Egypt, Moses and the Ten Commandments, Daniel and the lions' den, Jonah and the great fish.

The history, prophecies, and events of the Old Testament reveal a loving God who continually calls His people back to Himself, no matter how much they rebel or fall away from Him. God's loving pursuit culminates with a plan to pay the penalty of sin for all time for all people. There are prophecies about a future Savior, called the Messiah, who would come to save people and bring justice and righteousness to a broken world. This Savior would be born a man but would still be God. Thus God Himself would come to the earth in human form to be the final sacrifice for all sin.

The New Testament

THE NEW TESTAMENT tells about the birth of Jesus, the long-awaited Savior, His life on earth, His death, His resurrection, and the spread of the Good News of eternal salvation. The book of Acts tells the story of the coming of the Holy Spirit and the growth of the early church. The New Testament includes letters written by Jesus' followers, mainly the apostle Paul, to various churches and those seeking to live the Christian life in the initial years after Jesus' death and resurrection. In these letters we find practical wisdom, teaching, and encouragement for living as followers of Jesus in a non-Christian world. The last book of the Bible, Revelation, is a prophecy about the future return of Jesus Christ when He will come again and set up His eternal kingdom (Revelation was also written by John, at the end of his life, while he was in exile).

The Gospels

THE FIRST FOUR books in the New Testament are called "Gospels," which means "Good News." And they are indeed good news, for they tell the story of Jesus' life, His teachings, His miracles, His death on our behalf, and His resurrection. Why are there four Gospels? Each writer had his own unique perspective and each was considering a different audience as he recorded Jesus' life. This would be like your family members telling their friends about a recent family vacation. Each person was in the same locations, but each would remember different aspects of what happened there depending on his or her own personality and the particular audience to whom each was talking.

Likewise, each Gospel writer tells the story of Jesus but with different perspectives on various events and details. Some events are recorded in all four Gospels and some are recorded only by one writer.

Matthew was one of Jesus' disciples; he was a Jew and a tax collector by profession. Matthew wrote mainly to his fellow Jews, encouraging them to see Jesus as their long-awaited Messiah (Savior).

Mark was a young Jewish man who was also one of Jesus' followers, although not one of the twelve disciples. Mark wrote to a Roman audience (non-Jewish), wanting to prove to them that Jesus was both the Jewish Messiah as well as the Savior of the whole world.

Luke was a Gentile (meaning he was not Jewish) and a doctor. He traveled with the apostle Paul and also wrote the book of Acts. Luke wanted all those who were not Jews to understand that Jesus lived and died for them as well.

John was one of Jesus' twelve disciples (like Matthew, one of the other Gospel writers). Writing his Gospel later than the others, John wanted to refute some of the teachings of the day that said Jesus was not really God. Throughout his Gospel, John makes it clear that Jesus was truly God and truly man.

A Note on Translations

THE ORIGINAL SCRIPTURES contained in the Bible were written in several ancient languages. The Old Testament began as an oral history and then was recorded in Hebrew and some portions in Aramaic, the languages of the Hebrew people. The New Testament was written primarily in Greek, the dominant language of the time. Modern Bibles have been translated by teams of scholars from the original languages, and numerous translations are available. This Gospel of John is in the New International Version, published in 1984. It is good to look at different translations of the Bible to see what is most comfortable for you, as well as be aware that there are slight variations in words and phrases, depending on which translation you are using. Regardless of the differences in the Bible translations, all of them tell the same stories and have the same content. All of them are God's inspired Word.

The Format

EACH BOOK OF the Bible is divided into chapters and verses. These make it easy to locate an exact section or sentence quickly. John 3:16, for example, means "the Gospel of John, chapter 3, verse 16." Some verses, like this one, are very well known; many people have memorized John 3:16 and can recite it by heart. Why? The whole message of the New Testament could almost be summed up in this one verse from John: "For God so loved the world that he gave his one and only Son, that whoever believes in him shall not perish but have eternal life."

Turn the page and begin the Gospel of John, the unique perspective from a man who walked with Jesus during the three years of His ministry on earth.

JESUS DID many other miraculous signs in the **presence of his disciples,**

which are not recorded in this book.

But **these are written** that you may *believe*

that JESUS is the Christ, **the SON of God,**

and that by believing

YOU MAY HAVE LIFE in his name.

John 20:30–31

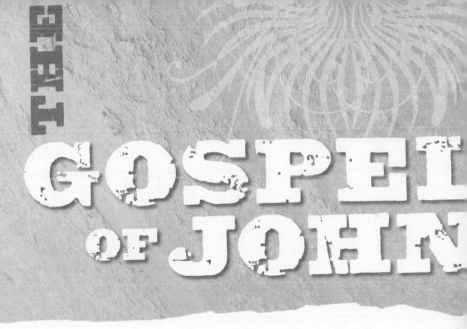

THE GOSPEL OF JOHN

At the end of his Gospel, John wrote that while Jesus did many miraculous signs in the presence of His disciples, "these are written that you may believe" (John 20:31, page 53). John's reason for recording this report of the Jesus he had known so well was to establish Jesus' true identity and to enable others to put their trust and confidence in Him.

John Who?
John was one of Jesus' twelve closest followers (disciples), along with his brother James. John appears in his own story several times, but not by name. At times you'll see a reference to "the disciple whom Jesus loved"—this is John, the author of this book! John knew Jesus loved him, and so described himself in this way. Of course, Jesus loved all of His disciples; John just made a special point of his knowledge of Jesus' love for him personally.

John had been a fisherman. In fact, when Jesus called John to follow Him, he was sitting in a boat on the edge of the Sea of Galilee with his father and brother, repairing the nets they used for fishing. John and his brother immediately responded and followed this man whom they came to recognize as the Messiah (the long-awaited Savior).

What's It All About?
As you begin reading this Gospel, you'll see that it doesn't at first read like a narrative. It has somewhat mysterious language about the "Word," and the "Word was God," and the "Word became flesh." The first eighteen verses serve as a kind of introduction, helping us to grasp that this upcoming story is not about an ordinary man, a good man, or even a great teacher. Instead, this Jesus is unlike any other; He is an eternal being, God in the flesh, who came to live among us.

John's Gospel begins when Jesus is already a grown man, about thirty years old. The familiar Christmas stories of Jesus' birth with Mary, Joseph, and wise men, are not written here—they are found in two of the other Gospels, Matthew and Luke. John's Gospel begins when Jesus was about to start His earthly ministry.

Another John?

The person you will read about first, in verse 19, is also named John, but he is not the author of this book. This is John the Baptist, a man who went through the countryside preaching that the Savior was coming. John the Baptist called people to be baptized (immersed in water) as a sign of turning away from sin as they anticipated the Savior's arrival. When Jesus is first introduced in verse 29, John recognized Him immediately and said, "Look, the Lamb of God, who takes away the sin of the world!" (see explanation of the term "Lamb of God" on page 4).

Interesting Tidbit

Another Gospel, the one written by Mark, has a little side note in its list of Jesus' disciples explaining that Jesus gave the nickname "Sons of Thunder" to the brothers James and John. Perhaps they were impetuous and hot tempered? Isn't it interesting that Jesus' disciples were not perfect people? It seems that despite our flaws God knows what He's getting when He calls us, and He loves us anyway.

A Snapshot of the Time

Jesus was born in what is now called the Middle East, in the countryside outside of Jerusalem—the same Jerusalem that exists today. It was the time of the Roman Empire, so the entire region was governed by Roman officials.

John's account takes place almost two thousand years ago—please note that our modern Western calendar begins with the year Jesus was born. The calendar prior to that, everything that took place in the Old Testament, is now referred to as B.C. ("Before Christ").

Jesus was born and raised in a Jewish community and was therefore very familiar with the scriptures that we now call the Old Testament. He went to the local synagogue and to the temple in Jerusalem, celebrated the Jewish holidays (feasts), and both learned from and debated with the religious leaders of His day.

It is important to note that when Jesus referred to "the Scriptures" in John's Gospel, His Jewish audience would have known what He was referring to in a way that might be unfamiliar to us. For Jesus to point to the sections of their own Scripture (what we call the Old Testament) that predicted the coming of the Messiah and to then say that He was the man who fulfilled the prophecies would have been quite shocking and scandalous! How could an ordinary man, a carpenter's son from a small village called Nazareth, be the prophesied Savior? No one expected that . . .

THE GOSPEL OF JOHN AT A GLANCE

WHO: John, one of Jesus' twelve disciples (his brother James was also one of Jesus' twelve disciples).

WHAT: The story of Jesus' life and an argument for Jesus being divine and the only One through whom we can have salvation.

WHEN: Written toward the end of the first century A.D. This was after the Romans destroyed Jerusalem (70 A.D.) but before they exiled John to an island in the Aegean Sea as punishment for preaching about Jesus.

WHERE: Unknown.

WHY: To prove that Jesus is the Son of God and that by believing in Him we can have eternal life.

GOD BECAME HUMAN

1 In the beginning was the Word, and the Word was with God, and the Word was God. ²He was with God in the beginning.

³Through him all things were made; without him nothing was made that has been made. ⁴In him was life, and that life was the light of men. ⁵The light shines in the darkness, but the darkness has not understood[a] it.

⁶There came a man who was sent from God; his name was John. ⁷He came as a witness to testify concerning that light, so that through him all men might believe. ⁸He himself was not the light; he came only as a witness to the light. ⁹The true light that gives light to every man was coming into the world.[b]

¹⁰He was in the world, and though the world was made through him, the world did not recognize him. ¹¹He came to that which was his own, but his own did not receive him. ¹²Yet to all who received him, to those who believed in his name, he gave the right to become children of God— ¹³children born not of natural descent,[c] nor of human decision or a husband's will, but born of God.

¹⁴The Word became flesh and made his dwelling among us. We have seen his glory, the glory of the One and Only,[d] who came from the Father, full of grace and truth.

¹⁵John testifies concerning him. He cries out, saying, "This was he of whom I said, 'He who comes after me has surpassed me because he was before me.'" ¹⁶From the fullness of his grace we have all received one blessing after another. ¹⁷For the law was given through Moses; grace and truth came through Jesus Christ. ¹⁸No one has ever seen God, but God the One and Only,[d,e] who is at the Father's side, has made him known.

---

[a]5 Or *darkness, and the darkness has not overcome*   [b]9 Or *This was the true light that gives light to every man who comes into the world*   [c]13 Greek *of bloods*   [d]14, 18 Or *the Only Begotten*   [e]18 Some manuscripts *but the only (or only begotten) Son*

JOHN THE BAPTIST TELLS HIS PURPOSE

[19]Now this was John's testimony when the Jews of Jerusalem sent priests and Levites to ask him who he was. [20]He did not fail to confess, but confessed freely, "I am not the Christ.[a]"

[21]They asked him, "Then who are you? Are you Elijah?"

He said, "I am not."

"Are you the Prophet?"

He answered, "No."

[22]Finally they said, "Who are you? Give us an answer to take back to those who sent us. What do you say about yourself?"

[23]John replied in the words of Isaiah the prophet, "I am the voice of one calling in the desert, 'Make straight the way for the Lord.'"[b]

[24]Now some Pharisees who had been sent [25]questioned him, "Why then do you baptize if you are not the Christ, nor Elijah, nor the Prophet?"

[26]"I baptize with[c] water," John replied, "but among you stands one you do not know. [27]He is the one who comes after me, the thongs of whose sandals I am not worthy to untie."

[28]This all happened at Bethany on the other side of the Jordan, where John was baptizing.

JESUS IS THE LAMB OF GOD

[29]The next day John saw Jesus coming toward him and said, "Look, the Lamb of God, who takes away the sin of the world! [30]This is the one I meant when I said, 'A man who comes after me has surpassed me because he was before me.' [31]I myself did not know him, but the reason I came baptizing with water was that he might be revealed to Israel."

[32]Then John gave this testimony: "I saw the Spirit come down from heaven as a dove and remain on him. [33]I would not have known him, except that the one who sent me to baptize with water told me, 'The man on whom you see the Spirit come down and remain is he who will baptize with the Holy Spirit.' [34]I have seen and I testify that this is the Son of God."

WHAT IS THE LAMB OF GOD?

John the Baptist referred to Jesus as the "Lamb of God, who takes away the sin of the world." In Old Testament times, the Hebrew people sacrificed animals; the death of animals was a constant reminder of the serious penalty of sin—an animal died in place of the person. This was a picture of the coming sacrifice of the Lamb of God, Jesus, who came to die on behalf of all people's sin. He was the ultimate pure sacrifice, provided by God Himself.

THE FIRST DISCIPLES FOLLOW JESUS

[35]The next day John was there again with two of his disciples. [36]When he saw Jesus passing by, he said, "Look, the Lamb of God!"

[37]When the two disciples heard him say this, they followed Jesus. [38]Turning around, Jesus saw them following and asked, "What do you want?"

---

[a]20 Or *Messiah*. "The Christ" (Greek) and "the Messiah" (Hebrew) both mean "the Anointed One"; also in verse 25. [b]23 Isaiah 40:3 [c]26 Or *in*; also in verses 31 and 33

They said, "Rabbi" (which means Teacher), "where are you staying?"
39"Come," he replied, "and you will see."

So they went and saw where he was staying, and spent that day with him. It was about the tenth hour.

40Andrew, Simon Peter's brother, was one of the two who heard what John had said and who had followed Jesus. 41The first thing Andrew did was to find his brother Simon and tell him, "We have found the Messiah" (that is, the Christ). 42And he brought him to Jesus.

Jesus looked at him and said, "You are Simon son of John. You will be called Cephas" (which, when translated, is Peter*a*).

PHILIP AND NATHANAEL BELIEVE

43The next day Jesus decided to leave for Galilee. Finding Philip, he said to him, "Follow me."

44Philip, like Andrew and Peter, was from the town of Bethsaida. 45**Philip found Nathanael and told him, "We have found the one Moses wrote about in the Law, and about whom the prophets also wrote—Jesus of Nazareth, the son of Joseph."**

---

*a*42 Both *Cephas* (Aramaic) and *Peter* (Greek) mean *rock*.

JOHN 1:45

"We Have Found the One!"

PHILIP FOUND NATHANAEL and told him, "We have found the one Moses wrote about in the Law, and about whom the prophets also wrote—Jesus of Nazareth, the son of Joseph."

The Jewish people had been waiting for a Messiah, a Savior. The Scriptures (referred to as "the Law and the Prophets" by the Jews) foretold the coming Messiah, and the Jews were waiting eagerly for His arrival. No one was expecting this Savior to come from an unimportant place called Nazareth, however, so Nathanael exclaimed, "Nazareth! Can anything good come from there?"

Philip was a thoughtful man who had studied the Scriptures and was looking for the Messiah. Because he studied the ancient Scriptures (some of them more than a thousand years old by this time), Philip was prepared to recognize Jesus, the One for whom his people had been waiting for centuries.

The message of Christianity is to "come and see" whom we have found. The Bible, God's Word, offers the same invitation: Come and see Jesus and know why Philip was so excited.

⁴⁶"Nazareth! Can anything good come from there?" Nathanael asked. "Come and see," said Philip.

⁴⁷When Jesus saw Nathanael approaching, he said of him, "Here is a true Israelite, in whom there is nothing false."

⁴⁸"How do you know me?" Nathanael asked.

Jesus answered, "I saw you while you were still under the fig tree before Philip called you."

⁴⁹Then Nathanael declared, "Rabbi, you are the Son of God; you are the King of Israel."

⁵⁰Jesus said, "You believe*a* because I told you I saw you under the fig tree. You shall see greater things than that." ⁵¹He then added, "I tell you*b* the truth, you*b* shall see heaven open, and the angels of God ascending and descending on the Son of Man."

JESUS PERFORMS HIS FIRST MIRACLE

2 On the third day a wedding took place at Cana in Galilee. Jesus' mother was there, ²and Jesus and his disciples had also been invited to the wedding. ³When the wine was gone, Jesus' mother said to him, "They have no more wine."

⁴"Dear woman, why do you involve me?" Jesus replied. "My time has not yet come."

⁵His mother said to the servants, "Do whatever he tells you."

⁶Nearby stood six stone water jars, the kind used by the Jews for ceremonial washing, each holding from twenty to thirty gallons.*c*

⁷Jesus said to the servants, "Fill the jars with water"; so they filled them to the brim.

⁸Then he told them, "Now draw some out and take it to the master of the banquet."

They did so, ⁹and the master of the banquet tasted the water that had been turned into wine. He did not realize where it had come from, though the servants who had drawn the water knew. Then he called the bridegroom aside ¹⁰and said, "Everyone brings out the choice wine first and then the cheaper wine after the guests have had too much to drink; but you have saved the best till now."

¹¹This, the first of his miraculous signs, Jesus performed at Cana in Galilee. He thus revealed his glory, and his disciples put their faith in him.

JESUS' RIGHTEOUS ANGER

¹²After this he went down to Capernaum with his mother and brothers and his disciples. There they stayed for a few days.

¹³When it was almost time for the Jewish Passover, Jesus went up to Jerusalem. ¹⁴In the temple courts he found men selling cattle, sheep and doves, and others sitting at tables exchanging money. ¹⁵So he made a whip

---

*a*50 Or *Do you believe…?*   *b*51 The Greek is plural.   *c*6 Greek *two to three metretes* (probably about 75 to 115 liters)

out of cords, and drove all from the temple area, both sheep and cattle; he scattered the coins of the money changers and overturned their tables. [16]To those who sold doves he said, "Get these out of here! How dare you turn my Father's house into a market!"

[17]His disciples remembered that it is written: "Zeal for your house will consume me."[a]

[18]Then the Jews demanded of him, "What miraculous sign can you show us to prove your authority to do all this?"

[19]Jesus answered them, "Destroy this temple, and I will raise it again in three days."

[20]The Jews replied, "It has taken forty-six years to build this temple, and you are going to raise it in three days?" [21]But the temple he had spoken of was his body. [22]After he was raised from the dead, his disciples recalled what he had said. Then they believed the Scripture and the words that Jesus had spoken.

[23]Now while he was in Jerusalem at the Passover Feast, many people saw the miraculous signs he was doing and believed in his name.[b] [24]But Jesus would not entrust himself to them, for he knew all men. [25]He did not need man's testimony about man, for he knew what was in a man.

JESUS TELLS THE WAY TO GOD

3 Now there was a man of the Pharisees named Nicodemus, a member of the Jewish ruling council. [2]He came to Jesus at night and said, "Rabbi, we know you are a teacher who has come from God. For no one could perform the miraculous signs you are doing if God were not with him."

[3]In reply Jesus declared, "I tell you the truth, no one can see the kingdom of God unless he is born again.[c]"

[4]"How can a man be born when he is old?" Nicodemus asked. "Surely he cannot enter a second time into his mother's womb to be born!"

[5]Jesus answered, "I tell you the truth, no one can enter the kingdom of God unless he is born of water and the Spirit. [6]Flesh gives birth to flesh, but the Spirit[d] gives birth to spirit. [7]You should not be surprised at my saying, 'You[e] must be born again.' [8]The wind blows wherever it pleases. You hear its sound, but you cannot tell where it comes from or where it is going. So it is with everyone born of the Spirit."

WHAT DOES IT MEAN TO BE "BORN AGAIN"?

Jesus told Nicodemus, "No one can see the kingdom of God unless he is born again." Jesus was not referring to being physically born again, but rather to a spiritual birth. He said, "Flesh gives birth to flesh, but the Spirit gives birth to spirit" (3:6). In order to see God's kingdom, we must allow a new life to begin in us. We receive this life from God by trusting in Him. There are many modern connotations associated with the phrase "born again," but Jesus was actually the first to speak these words.

---

[a]17 Psalm 69:9   [b]23 Or *and believed in him*   [c]3 Or *born from above*; also in verse 7   [d]6 Or *but spirit*
[e]7 The Greek is plural.

⁹"How can this be?" Nicodemus asked.

¹⁰"You are Israel's teacher," said Jesus, "and do you not understand these things? ¹¹I tell you the truth, we speak of what we know, and we testify to what we have seen, but still you people do not accept our testimony. ¹²I have spoken to you of earthly things and you do not believe; how then will you believe if I speak of heavenly things? ¹³No one has ever gone into heaven except the one who came from heaven—the Son of Man.ᵃ ¹⁴Just as Moses lifted up the snake in the desert, so the Son of Man must be lifted up, ¹⁵that everyone who believes in him may have eternal life.ᵇ

¹⁶"For God so loved the world that he gave his one and only Son,ᶜ that whoever believes in him shall not perish but have eternal life. ¹⁷For God did not send his Son into the world to condemn the world, but to save the world through him. ¹⁸Whoever believes in him is not condemned, but whoever does not believe stands condemned already because he has not believed in the name of God's one and only Son.ᵈ ¹⁹This is the verdict: Light has come into the world, but men loved darkness instead of light because their deeds were evil. ²⁰Everyone who does evil hates the light, and will not come into the light for fear that his deeds will be exposed. ²¹But whoever lives by the truth comes into the light, so that it may be seen plainly that what he has done has been done through God."ᵉ

JOHN THE BAPTIST TELLS ABOUT JESUS

²²After this, Jesus and his disciples went out into the Judean country-side, where he spent some time with them, and baptized. ²³Now John

ᵃ13 Some manuscripts *Man, who is in heaven*   ᵇ15 Or *believes may have eternal life in him*   ᶜ16 Or *his only begotten Son*   ᵈ18 Or *God's only begotten Son*   ᵉ21 Some interpreters end the quotation after verse 15.

JOHN 3:31-35

The Words of God

JOHN THE BAPTIST explained to his audience that he himself was not the Messiah; instead, he was a prophet pointing the way. He said of the coming Messiah, "The one whom God has sent speaks the words of God, for God gives the Spirit without limit."

"The Spirit" (the Holy Spirit) spoke through the prophets in the Old Testament. These prophets received the Holy Spirit only periodically, however, when they were talking with or for God. Because Jesus is God in human form, He is able to speak the words of God directly. Jesus is the *living* Word—He not only spoke the truth but also demonstrated it with His life.

Today God still speaks to His people through Jesus (by His Spirit) and through His words in the Bible.

also was baptizing at Aenon near Salim, because there was plenty of water, and people were constantly coming to be baptized. ²⁴(This was before John was put in prison.) ²⁵An argument developed between some of John's disciples and a certain Jew[a] over the matter of ceremonial washing. ²⁶They came to John and said to him, "Rabbi, that man who was with you on the other side of the Jordan—the one you testified about—well, he is baptizing, and everyone is going to him."

²⁷To this John replied, "A man can receive only what is given him from heaven. ²⁸You yourselves can testify that I said, 'I am not the Christ[b] but am sent ahead of him.' ²⁹The bride belongs to the bridegroom. The friend who attends the bridegroom waits and listens for him, and is full of joy when he hears the bridegroom's voice. That joy is mine, and it is now complete. ³⁰He must become greater; I must become less.

³¹**"The one who comes from above is above all; the one who is from the earth belongs to the earth, and speaks as one from the earth. The one who comes from heaven is above all. ³²He testifies to what he has seen and heard, but no one accepts his testimony. ³³The man who has accepted it has certified that God is truthful. ³⁴For the one whom God has sent speaks the words of God, for God[c] gives the Spirit without limit. ³⁵The Father loves the Son and has placed everything in his hands.** ³⁶Whoever believes in the Son has eternal life, but whoever rejects the Son will not see life, for God's wrath remains on him."[d]

JESUS TALKS WITH A SAMARITAN WOMAN

4 The Pharisees heard that Jesus was gaining and baptizing more disciples than John, ²although in fact it was not Jesus who baptized, but his disciples. ³When the Lord learned of this, he left Judea and went back once more to Galilee.

⁴Now he had to go through Samaria. ⁵So he came to a town in Samaria called Sychar, near the plot of ground Jacob had given to his son Joseph. ⁶Jacob's well was there, and Jesus, tired as he was from the journey, sat down by the well. It was about the sixth hour.

⁷When a Samaritan woman came to draw water, Jesus said to her, "Will you give me a drink?" ⁸(His disciples had gone into the town to buy food.)

⁹The Samaritan woman said to him, "You are a Jew and I am a Samaritan woman. How can you ask me for a drink?" (For Jews do not associate with Samaritans.[e])

WHO WERE THE SAMARITANS?

The Samaritans were a mixed-Jewish race and, as John pointed out, the "pure" Jews would not associate with them. In addition, men did not usually speak to women in public. For a Jewish man to speak to a Samaritan woman alone, as Jesus did, was quite scandalous. In this event, Jesus demonstrated that His message is for all people, the rejected and the outcast alike, and not just for His own race.

---

[a]25 Some manuscripts *and certain Jews* [b]28 Or *Messiah* [c]34 Greek *he* [d]36 Some interpreters end the quotation after verse 30. [e]9 Or *do not use dishes Samaritans have used*

¹⁰Jesus answered her, "If you knew the gift of God and who it is that asks you for a drink, you would have asked him and he would have given you living water."

¹¹"Sir," the woman said, "you have nothing to draw with and the well is deep. Where can you get this living water? ¹²Are you greater than our father Jacob, who gave us the well and drank from it himself, as did also his sons and his flocks and herds?"

¹³Jesus answered, "Everyone who drinks this water will be thirsty again, ¹⁴but whoever drinks the water I give him will never thirst. Indeed, the water I give him will become in him a spring of water welling up to eternal life."

¹⁵The woman said to him, "Sir, give me this water so that I won't get thirsty and have to keep coming here to draw water."

¹⁶He told her, "Go, call your husband and come back."

¹⁷"I have no husband," she replied.

Jesus said to her, "You are right when you say you have no husband. ¹⁸The fact is, you have had five husbands, and the man you now have is not your husband. What you have just said is quite true."

¹⁹"Sir," the woman said, "I can see that you are a prophet. ²⁰Our fathers worshiped on this mountain, but you Jews claim that the place where we must worship is in Jerusalem."

²¹Jesus declared, "Believe me, woman, a time is coming when you will worship the Father neither on this mountain nor in Jerusalem. ²²You Samaritans worship what you do not know; we worship what we do know, for salvation is from the Jews. ²³Yet a time is coming and has now come when the true worshipers will worship the Father in spirit and truth, for they are the kind of worshipers the Father seeks. ²⁴God is spirit, and his worshipers must worship in spirit and in truth."

²⁵The woman said, "I know that Messiah" (called Christ) "is coming. When he comes, he will explain everything to us."

²⁶Then Jesus declared, "I who speak to you am he."

THE DISCIPLES REJOIN JESUS

²⁷Just then his disciples returned and were surprised to find him talking with a woman. But no one asked, "What do you want?" or "Why are you talking with her?"

²⁸Then, leaving her water jar, the woman went back to the town and said to the people, ²⁹"Come, see a man who told me everything I ever did. Could this be the Christ[a]?" ³⁰They came out of the town and made their way toward him.

³¹Meanwhile his disciples urged him, "Rabbi, eat something."

³²But he said to them, "I have food to eat that you know nothing about."

³³Then his disciples said to each other, "Could someone have brought him food?"

[a]29 Or *Messiah*

³⁴"My food," said Jesus, "is to do the will of him who sent me and to finish his work. ³⁵Do you not say, 'Four months more and then the harvest'? I tell you, open your eyes and look at the fields! They are ripe for harvest. ³⁶Even now the reaper draws his wages, even now he harvests the crop for eternal life, so that the sower and the reaper may be glad together. ³⁷Thus the saying 'One sows and another reaps' is true. ³⁸I sent you to reap what you have not worked for. Others have done the hard work, and you have reaped the benefits of their labor."

MANY SAMARITANS BELIEVE

³⁹Many of the Samaritans from that town believed in him because of the woman's testimony, "He told me everything I ever did." ⁴⁰So when the Samaritans came to him, they urged him to stay with them, and he stayed two days. ⁴¹And because of his words many more became believers.

⁴²They said to the woman, "We no longer believe just because of what you said; now we have heard for ourselves, and we know that this man really is the Savior of the world."

JESUS HEALS THE OFFICIAL'S SON

⁴³After the two days he left for Galilee. ⁴⁴(Now Jesus himself had pointed out that a prophet has no honor in his own country.) ⁴⁵When he arrived in Galilee, the Galileans welcomed him. They had seen all that he had done in Jerusalem at the Passover Feast, for they also had been there.

⁴⁶Once more he visited Cana in Galilee, where he had turned the water into wine. And there was a certain royal official whose son lay sick at Capernaum. ⁴⁷When this man heard that Jesus had arrived in Galilee from Judea, he went to him and begged him to come and heal his son, who was close to death.

⁴⁸"Unless you people see miraculous signs and wonders," Jesus told him, "you will never believe."

⁴⁹The royal official said, "Sir, come down before my child dies."

⁵⁰Jesus replied, "You may go. Your son will live."

The man took Jesus at his word and departed. ⁵¹While he was still on the way, his servants met him with the news that his boy was living. ⁵²When he inquired as to the time when his son got better, they said to him, "The fever left him yesterday at the seventh hour."

⁵³Then the father realized that this was the exact time at which Jesus had said to him, "Your son will live." So he and all his household believed.

⁵⁴This was the second miraculous sign that Jesus performed, having come from Judea to Galilee.

JESUS HEALS A PARALYZED MAN

5 Some time later, Jesus went up to Jerusalem for a feast of the Jews. ²Now there is in Jerusalem near the Sheep Gate a pool, which in Aramaic is called Bethesda*ᵃ* and which is surrounded by five covered colonnades. ³Here

---

ᵃ2 Some manuscripts Bethzatha; other manuscripts Bethsaida

a great number of disabled people used to lie—the blind, the lame, the paralyzed.[a] 5One who was there had been an invalid for thirty-eight years. 6When
Jesus saw him lying there and learned that he had been in this condition for
a long time, he asked him, "Do you want to get well?"

7"Sir," the invalid replied, "I have no one to help me into the pool when the
water is stirred. While I am trying to get in, someone else goes down ahead
of me."

8Then Jesus said to him, "Get up! Pick up your mat and walk." 9At once
the man was cured; he picked up his mat and walked.

The day on which this took place was a Sabbath, 10and so the Jews said
to the man who had been healed, "It is the Sabbath; the law forbids you
to carry your mat."

11But he replied, "The man who made me well said to me, 'Pick up your
mat and walk.'"

12So they asked him, "Who is this fellow who told you to pick it up
and walk?"

13The man who was healed had no idea who it was, for Jesus had
slipped away into the crowd that was there.

14Later Jesus found him at the temple and said to him, "See, you are well
again. Stop sinning or something worse may happen to you." 15The man
went away and told the Jews that it was Jesus who had made him well.

FINDING LIFE THROUGH JESUS

16So, because Jesus was doing these things on the Sabbath, the Jews
persecuted him. 17Jesus said to them, "My Father is always at his work to
this very day, and I, too, am working." 18For this reason the Jews tried all
the harder to kill him; not only was he breaking the Sabbath, but he was
even calling God his own Father, making himself equal with God.

19Jesus gave them this answer: "I tell you the truth, the Son can do
nothing by himself; he can do only what he sees his Father doing, because
whatever the Father does the Son also does. 20For the Father loves the
Son and shows him all he does. Yes, to your amazement he will show him
even greater things than these. 21For just as the Father raises the dead and
gives them life, even so the Son gives life to whom he is pleased to give
it. 22Moreover, the Father judges no one, but has entrusted all judgment
to the Son, 23that all may honor the Son just as they honor the Father. He
who does not honor the Son does not honor the Father, who sent him.

24"I tell you the truth, whoever hears my word and believes him who
sent me has eternal life and will not be condemned; he has crossed over
from death to life. 25I tell you the truth, a time is coming and has now
come when the dead will hear the voice of the Son of God and those who
hear will live. 26For as the Father has life in himself, so he has granted the

---

[a]3 Some less important manuscripts paralyzed—and they waited for the moving of the waters. 'From time
to time an angel of the Lord would come down and stir up the waters. The first one into the pool after each
such disturbance would be cured of whatever disease he had.

Son to have life in himself. [27]And he has given him authority to judge because he is the Son of Man.

[28]"Do not be amazed at this, for a time is coming when all who are in their graves will hear his voice [29]and come out—those who have done good will rise to live, and those who have done evil will rise to be condemned. [30]By myself I can do nothing; I judge only as I hear, and my judgment is just, for I seek not to please myself but him who sent me.

TESTIMONIES ABOUT JESUS

[31]"If I testify about myself, my testimony is not valid. [32]There is another who testifies in my favor, and I know that his testimony about me is valid. [33]"You have sent to John and he has testified to the truth. [34]Not that I accept human testimony; but I mention it that you may be saved. [35]John was a lamp that burned and gave light, and you chose for a time to enjoy his light.

[36]"I have testimony weightier than that of John. For the very work that the Father has given me to finish, and which I am doing, testifies that the Father has sent me. [37]And the Father who sent me has himself testified concerning me. You have never heard his voice nor seen his form, [38]nor does his word dwell in you, for you do not believe the one he sent. [39]**You diligently study*[a]* the Scriptures because you think that by them you possess eternal life. These are the Scriptures that testify about me, [40]yet you refuse to come to me to have life.**

[41]"I do not accept praise from men, [42]but I know you. I know that you

---

[a]39 Or *Study diligently* (the imperative)

JOHN 5:39-40

The Source of Life

IN JESUS' DAY, scholars thought they could possess eternal life by continually studying and analyzing the holy Scriptures. These men knew what Scripture said, but they often didn't apply its principles to their lives. Many were so caught up in religious study and arguments that they missed the Messiah Himself. That's why Jesus said, "You diligently study the Scriptures because you think that by them you possess eternal life. These are the Scriptures that testify about me, yet you refuse to come to me to have life."

People can spend hours reading the Bible and underlining various passages. But real life comes from having a personal relationship with Jesus, not just from reading the Bible. That personal relationship requires time spent with Jesus and time reading God's Word. The purpose of Bible study should be to search for, find, and learn about Jesus. The Bible isn't just a book of rules; it is a map and a guide that lead to Christ as the source of life.

do not have the love of God in your hearts. [43]I have come in my Father's name, and you do not accept me; but if someone else comes in his own name, you will accept him. [44]How can you believe if you accept praise from one another, yet make no effort to obtain the praise that comes from the only God[a]?

[45]"But do not think I will accuse you before the Father. Your accuser is Moses, on whom your hopes are set. [46]If you believed Moses, you would believe me, for he wrote about me. [47]But since you do not believe what he wrote, how are you going to believe what I say?"

JESUS FEEDS OVER FIVE THOUSAND PEOPLE

6 Some time after this, Jesus crossed to the far shore of the Sea of Galilee (that is, the Sea of Tiberias), [2]and a great crowd of people followed him because they saw the miraculous signs he had performed on the sick. [3]Then Jesus went up on a mountainside and sat down with his disciples. [4]The Jewish Passover Feast was near.

[5]When Jesus looked up and saw a great crowd coming toward him, he said to Philip, "Where shall we buy bread for these people to eat?" [6]He asked this only to test him, for he already had in mind what he was going to do.

[7]Philip answered him, "Eight months' wages[b] would not buy enough bread for each one to have a bite!"

[8]Another of his disciples, Andrew, Simon Peter's brother, spoke up, [9]"Here is a boy with five small barley loaves and two small fish, but how far will they go among so many?"

[10]Jesus said, "Have the people sit down." There was plenty of grass in that place, and the men sat down, about five thousand of them. [11]Jesus then took the loaves, gave thanks, and distributed to those who were seated as much as they wanted. He did the same with the fish.

[12]When they had all had enough to eat, he said to his disciples, "Gather the pieces that are left over. Let nothing be wasted." [13]So they gathered them and filled twelve baskets with the pieces of the five barley loaves left over by those who had eaten.

[14]After the people saw the miraculous sign that Jesus did, they began to say, "Surely this is the Prophet who is to come into the world." [15]Jesus, knowing that they intended to come and make him king by force, withdrew again to a mountain by himself.

JESUS WALKS ON THE WATER

[16]When evening came, his disciples went down to the lake, [17]where they got into a boat and set off across the lake for Capernaum. By now it was dark, and Jesus had not yet joined them. [18]A strong wind was blowing and the waters grew rough. [19]When they had rowed three or three and a half miles,[c]

---

[a]44 Some early manuscripts *the Only One*   [b]7 Greek *two hundred denarii*   [c]19 Greek *rowed twenty-five or thirty stadia* (about 5 or 6 kilometers)

they saw Jesus approaching the boat, walking on the water; and they were terrified. [20]But he said to them, "It is I; don't be afraid." [21]Then they were willing to take him into the boat, and immediately the boat reached the shore where they were heading.

[22]The next day the crowd that had stayed on the opposite shore of the lake realized that only one boat had been there, and that Jesus had not entered it with his disciples, but that they had gone away alone. [23]Then some boats from Tiberias landed near the place where the people had eaten the bread after the Lord had given thanks. [24]Once the crowd realized that neither Jesus nor his disciples were there, they got into the boats and went to Capernaum in search of Jesus.

JESUS IS THE BREAD OF LIFE

[25]When they found him on the other side of the lake, they asked him, "Rabbi, when did you get here?"

[26]Jesus answered, "I tell you the truth, you are looking for me, not because you saw miraculous signs but because you ate the loaves and had your fill. [27]Do not work for food that spoils, but for food that endures to eternal life, which the Son of Man will give you. On him God the Father has placed his seal of approval."

[28]Then they asked him, "What must we do to do the works God requires?"

[29]Jesus answered, "The work of God is this: to believe in the one he has sent."

[30]So they asked him, "What miraculous sign then will you give that we may see it and believe you? What will you do? [31]Our forefathers ate the manna in the desert; as it is written: 'He gave them bread from heaven to eat.'[a]"

[32]Jesus said to them, "I tell you the truth, it is not Moses who has given you the bread from heaven, but it is my Father who gives you the true bread from heaven. [33]For the bread of God is he who comes down from heaven and gives life to the world."

[34]"Sir," they said, "from now on give us this bread."

[35]Then Jesus declared, "I am the bread of life. He who comes to me will never go hungry, and he who believes in me will never be thirsty. [36]But as I told you, you have seen me and still you do not believe. [37]All that the Father gives me will come to me, and whoever comes to me I will never drive away. [38]For I have come down from heaven not to do my will but to do the will of him who sent me. [39]And this is the will of him who sent me, that I shall lose none of all that he has given me, but raise them up at the last day. [40]For my Father's will is that everyone who looks to the Son and believes in him shall have eternal life, and I will raise him up at the last day."

[41]At this the Jews began to grumble about him because he said, "I am the bread that came down from heaven." [42]They said, "Is this not Jesus,

a31 Exodus 16:4; Neh. 9:15; Psalm 78:24,25

FOR SOME PEOPLE, going to church has always been a part of life. They grew up attending church, but somehow missed out on the fact that church is about a personal relationship with Jesus Christ. Perhaps their church never taught them that, or perhaps they didn't hear it, or perhaps they heard it but chose not to respond. Every individual needs to come to Jesus personally. Nicole describes how the Alpha course brought her face to face with the question of her personal relationship with Jesus.

FINDING ANSWERS

NICOLE'S STORY

I was raised going to church on Sundays, but that was about it. My parents did not have a "Christian" home. When I moved out of their house after college, I thought, *Wahoo! I have an extra hour on Sundays now!* So I abandoned the church and tried other things instead. At the time, I wouldn't have said I needed God, but nothing satisfied me. When I moved to California, my grandma said I should find a church, but I told her, "Church is your thing, not mine."

I moved to San Jose in April 2001. I remember thinking, *I should be feeling happy!* but I wasn't. The first month there, I got a newsletter from a nearby church. I wasn't looking for God, but I suppose you could say He found me in my mailbox. I read the whole thing, front to back. I was looking for connection, community, and friendship. Church had always seemed like something people did for an hour on Sundays but that didn't affect the rest of the week. So I was a bit surprised to find myself wanting to go to church. The next Sunday morning, I put on a dress, got in the car, and thought, *I'm going to church today. Isn't that cute?*

I was pleasantly surprised. I really liked the music and the people. My impression was, "Wow! I don't know what it is, but these people really believe this stuff." They were excited to be there. That first Sunday, I signed up for the Singles group, then I got involved in everything I could. Church suddenly was no longer just for an hour on Sundays—and I was *glad* about that!

One of the groups I joined was called Alpha. I didn't know anything about Jesus or faith, and I wanted to ask questions. The flyer said that Alpha would give me that opportunity. I didn't realize that it was a class with a beginning and an end, I thought it was more like a youth group . . . so I didn't actually start going to Alpha until halfway through the course.

I really liked the format. I liked hearing Nicky Gumbel talk. In fact, I took the course again because I wanted to take the whole thing through without missing anything. You might think it would be boring to repeat, but when you've never heard this stuff before, it's fascinating. I wrote all over my book, writing down everything I heard. I love to ask lots of questions. During the discussion time I chimed right in, bringing up the notes I had written in the margins and asking my questions. At Alpha, no one was shocked or upset by my questions. They didn't care that I didn't know anything. They were patient. It was comfortable, safe, and I didn't feel stupid.

I became a Christian during the Alpha course. There was a little pamphlet that talked about how to become a Christian. I took it home, got down on my knees, and asked Jesus to come into my heart. Before that day my approach had always been, "Once I understand everything, then I'll become a Christian." But during Alpha I realized that I was never going to understand everything—in fact, that wasn't the goal. Instead, the goal was a relationship with a person named Jesus Christ. I never knew that church was about a relationship. That focus, that it was a personal thing, was new. It was about me, personally, understanding things, getting to know God, Jesus, and what the Bible had to say. I never, ever, had heard that in church before, but Alpha taught me that.

THEY WERE PATIENT. IT WAS COMFORTABLE, SAFE, AND I DIDN'T FEEL STUPID.

By the second time through the course, I actually started helping people answer the questions. When they started the next course, the leader asked me to be a table host. Now my best friend was at my table and I helped to introduce her to Christ! I was a table leader three more times after that. I am totally passionate about sharing this message and excited to help other people on that journey.

the son of Joseph, whose father and mother we know? How can he now say, 'I came down from heaven'?"

⁴³"Stop grumbling among yourselves," Jesus answered. ⁴⁴"No one can come to me unless the Father who sent me draws him, and I will raise him up at the last day. ⁴⁵It is written in the Prophets: 'They will all be taught by God.'ᵃ Everyone who listens to the Father and learns from him comes to me. ⁴⁶No one has seen the Father except the one who is from God; only he has seen the Father. ⁴⁷I tell you the truth, he who believes has everlasting life. ⁴⁸I am the bread of life. ⁴⁹Your forefathers ate the manna in the desert, yet they died. ⁵⁰But here is the bread that comes down from heaven, which a man may eat and not die. ⁵¹I am the living bread that came down from heaven. If anyone eats of this bread, he will live forever. This bread is my flesh, which I will give for the life of the world."

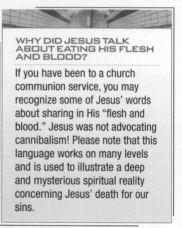

WHY DID JESUS TALK ABOUT EATING HIS FLESH AND BLOOD?

If you have been to a church communion service, you may recognize some of Jesus' words about sharing in His "flesh and blood." Jesus was not advocating cannibalism! Please note that this language works on many levels and is used to illustrate a deep and mysterious spiritual reality concerning Jesus' death for our sins.

⁵²Then the Jews began to argue sharply among themselves, "How can this man give us his flesh to eat?"

⁵³Jesus said to them, "I tell you the truth, unless you eat the flesh of the Son of Man and drink his blood, you have no life in you. ⁵⁴Whoever eats my flesh and drinks my blood has eternal life, and I will raise him up at the last day. ⁵⁵For my flesh is real food and my blood is real drink. ⁵⁶Whoever eats my flesh and drinks my blood remains in me, and I in him. ⁵⁷Just as the living Father sent me and I live because of the Father, so the one who feeds on me will live because of me. ⁵⁸This is the bread that came down from heaven. Your forefathers ate manna and died, but he who feeds on this bread will live forever." ⁵⁹He said this while teaching in the synagogue in Capernaum.

MANY DISCIPLES LEAVE JESUS

⁶⁰On hearing it, many of his disciples said, "This is a hard teaching. Who can accept it?"

⁶¹Aware that his disciples were grumbling about this, Jesus said to them, "Does this offend you? ⁶²What if you see the Son of Man ascend to where he was before! ⁶³The Spirit gives life; the flesh counts for nothing. The words I have spoken to you are spiritᵇ and they are life. ⁶⁴Yet there are some of you who do not believe." For Jesus had known from the beginning which of them did not believe and who would betray him. ⁶⁵He went on to say, "This is why I told you that no one can come to me unless the Father has enabled him."

ᵃ45 Isaiah 54:13   ᵇ63 Or *Spirit*

⁶⁶From this time many of his disciples turned back and no longer followed him.

⁶⁷"You do not want to leave too, do you?" Jesus asked the Twelve.

⁶⁸Simon Peter answered him, "Lord, to whom shall we go? You have the words of eternal life. ⁶⁹We believe and know that you are the Holy One of God."

⁷⁰Then Jesus replied, "Have I not chosen you, the Twelve? Yet one of you is a devil!" ⁷¹(He meant Judas, the son of Simon Iscariot, who, though one of the Twelve, was later to betray him.)

JESUS GOES TO THE FEAST OF TABERNACLES

7 After this, Jesus went around in Galilee, purposely staying away from Judea because the Jews there were waiting to take his life. ²But when the Jewish Feast of Tabernacles was near, ³Jesus' brothers said to him, "You ought to leave here and go to Judea, so that your disciples may see the miracles you do. ⁴No one who wants to become a public figure acts in secret. Since you are doing these things, show yourself to the world." ⁵For even his own brothers did not believe in him.

⁶Therefore Jesus told them, "The right time for me has not yet come; for you any time is right. ⁷The world cannot hate you, but it hates me because I testify that what it does is evil. ⁸You go to the Feast. I am not yet*ᵃ* going up to this Feast, because for me the right time has not yet come." ⁹Having said this, he stayed in Galilee.

¹⁰However, after his brothers had left for the Feast, he went also, not publicly, but in secret. ¹¹Now at the Feast the Jews were watching for him and asking, "Where is that man?"

¹²Among the crowds there was widespread whispering about him. Some said, "He is a good man."

Others replied, "No, he deceives the people." ¹³But no one would say anything publicly about him for fear of the Jews.

WHAT WAS THE FEAST OF TABERNACLES?

All of the Jewish feasts (holidays) originated from events described in the Old Testament. This particular feast celebrated how God had protected the people after their exodus from Egypt as they traveled in the desert. As a Jew, Jesus would have participated in these traditions, as many modern Jews still do today. You will find several feasts mentioned in the Gospels, such as Passover, which have significance both as existing Jewish holidays as well as events in Jesus' life. For example, the "Last Supper" was a Passover feast that Jesus celebrated with His disciples the night before His death.

JESUS TEACHES AT THE FEAST

¹⁴Not until halfway through the Feast did Jesus go up to the temple courts and begin to teach. ¹⁵The Jews were amazed and asked, "How did this man get such learning without having studied?"

¹⁶Jesus answered, "My teaching is not my own. It comes from him who

---

ᵃ8 Some early manuscripts do not have yet.

sent me. ¹⁷If anyone chooses to do God's will, he will find out whether my teaching comes from God or whether I speak on my own. ¹⁸He who speaks on his own does so to gain honor for himself, but he who works for the honor of the one who sent him is a man of truth; there is nothing false about him. ¹⁹Has not Moses given you the law? Yet not one of you keeps the law. Why are you trying to kill me?"

²⁰"You are demon-possessed," the crowd answered. "Who is trying to kill you?"

²¹Jesus said to them, "I did one miracle, and you are all astonished. ²²Yet, because Moses gave you circumcision (though actually it did not come from Moses, but from the patriarchs), you circumcise a child on the Sabbath. ²³Now if a child can be circumcised on the Sabbath so that the law of Moses may not be broken, why are you angry with me for healing the whole man on the Sabbath? ²⁴Stop judging by mere appearances, and make a right judgment."

WHAT WAS "BREAKING THE SABBATH"?

The Jewish Sabbath was a weekly day of rest during which people were to do no work of any kind. Because Jesus chose to heal people on the Sabbath, many religious leaders accused him of "working" and breaking God's law. Jesus exposed the hypocrisy of outwardly keeping the Sabbath while ignoring the needs of others. He showed that the spirit of the law is what is most important, and that while many "diligently study the Scriptures" (5:39) and seek to strictly follow the rules, they often miss the real point of God's instructions.

IS JESUS THE CHRIST?

²⁵At that point some of the people of Jerusalem began to ask, "Isn't this the man they are trying to kill? ²⁶Here he is, speaking publicly, and they are not saying a word to him. Have the authorities really concluded that he is the Christ*ᵃ*? ²⁷But we know where this man is from; when the Christ comes, no one will know where he is from."

²⁸Then Jesus, still teaching in the temple courts, cried out, "Yes, you know me, and you know where I am from. I am not here on my own, but he who sent me is true. You do not know him, ²⁹but I know him because I am from him and he sent me."

³⁰At this they tried to seize him, but no one laid a hand on him, because his time had not yet come. ³¹Still, many in the crowd put their faith in him. They said, "When the Christ comes, will he do more miraculous signs than this man?"

³²The Pharisees heard the crowd whispering such things about him. Then the chief priests and the Pharisees sent temple guards to arrest him.

³³Jesus said, "I am with you for only a short time, and then I go to the one who sent me. ³⁴You will look for me, but you will not find me; and where I am, you cannot come."

³⁵The Jews said to one another, "Where does this man intend to go that

---

*ᵃ*26 Or *Messiah*; also in verses 27, 31, 41 and 42

we cannot find him? Will he go where our people live scattered among the Greeks, and teach the Greeks? 36What did he mean when he said, 'You will look for me, but you will not find me,' and 'Where I am, you cannot come'?"

37On the last and greatest day of the Feast, Jesus stood and said in a loud voice, "If anyone is thirsty, let him come to me and drink. 38Whoever believes in me, as*a* the Scripture has said, streams of living water will flow from within him." 39By this he meant the Spirit, whom those who believed in him were later to receive. Up to that time the Spirit had not been given, since Jesus had not yet been glorified.

40On hearing his words, some of the people said, "Surely this man is the Prophet."

41Others said, "He is the Christ."

Still others asked, "How can the Christ come from Galilee? 42Does not the Scripture say that the Christ will come from David's family*b* and from Bethlehem, the town where David lived?" 43Thus the people were divided because of Jesus. 44Some wanted to seize him, but no one laid a hand on him.

UNBELIEF OF THE JEWISH LEADERS

45Finally the temple guards went back to the chief priests and Pharisees, who asked them, "Why didn't you bring him in?"

46"No one ever spoke the way this man does," the guards declared.

47"You mean he has deceived you also?" the Pharisees retorted. 48"Has any of the rulers or of the Pharisees believed in him? 49No! But this mob that knows nothing of the law—there is a curse on them."

50Nicodemus, who had gone to Jesus earlier and who was one of their own number, asked, 51"Does our law condemn anyone without first hearing him to find out what he is doing?"

52They replied, "Are you from Galilee, too? Look into it, and you will find that a prophet*c* does not come out of Galilee."

[The earliest manuscripts and many other ancient witnesses do not have John 7:53—8:11.]

53Then each went to his own home.

8 But Jesus went to the Mount of Olives. 2At dawn he appeared again in the temple courts, where all the people gathered around him, and he sat down to teach them. 3The teachers of the law and the Pharisees brought in a woman caught in adultery. They made her stand before the group 4and said to Jesus, "Teacher, this woman was caught in the act of adultery. 5In the Law Moses commanded us to stone such women. Now what do you say?" 6They were using this question as a trap, in order to have a basis for accusing him.

---

*a*37,38 Or / *If anyone is thirsty, let him come to me.* / *And let him drink, 38who believes in me.* / *As*
*b*42 Greek *seed*   *c*52 Two early manuscripts *the Prophet*

WHAT IS THE LAW OF MOSES?

God originally communicated His Law through Moses, by giving him the Ten Commandments. The Law grew in more detail from there (that's what you find in the Old Testament books of Exodus, Leviticus, and Deuteronomy). The Jews of Jesus' time used these laws as rules or guidelines for holy living, but many of the religious leaders also tried to catch Jesus breaking one of them. That way they would have grounds to have Him arrested.

But Jesus bent down and started to write on the ground with his finger. ⁷When they kept on questioning him, he straightened up and said to them, "If any one of you is without sin, let him be the first to throw a stone at her." ⁸Again he stooped down and wrote on the ground.

⁹At this, those who heard began to go away one at a time, the older ones first, until only Jesus was left, with the woman still standing there. ¹⁰Jesus straightened up and asked her, "Woman, where are they? Has no one condemned you?"

¹¹"No one, sir," she said.

"Then neither do I condemn you," Jesus declared. "Go now and leave your life of sin."

THE VALIDITY OF JESUS' TESTIMONY

¹²When Jesus spoke again to the people, he said, "I am the light of the world. Whoever follows me will never walk in darkness, but will have the light of life."

¹³The Pharisees challenged him, "Here you are, appearing as your own witness; your testimony is not valid."

¹⁴Jesus answered, "Even if I testify on my own behalf, my testimony is valid, for I know where I came from and where I am going. But you have no idea where I come from or where I am going. ¹⁵You judge by human standards; I pass judgment on no one. ¹⁶But if I do judge, my decisions are right, because I am not alone. I stand with the Father, who sent me. ¹⁷In your own Law it is written that the testimony of two men is valid. ¹⁸I am one who testifies for myself; my other witness is the Father, who sent me."

¹⁹Then they asked him, "Where is your father?"

"You do not know me or my Father," Jesus replied. "If you knew me, you would know my Father also." ²⁰He spoke these words while teaching in the temple area near the place where the offerings were put. Yet no one seized him, because his time had not yet come.

²¹Once more Jesus said to them, "I am going away, and you will look for me, and you will die in your sin. Where I go, you cannot come."

²²This made the Jews ask, "Will he kill himself? Is that why he says, 'Where I go, you cannot come'?"

²³But he continued, "You are from below; I am from above. You are of this world; I am not of this world. ²⁴I told you that you would die in your sins; if you do not believe that I am ⌞the one I claim to be⌟,ᵃ you will indeed die in your sins."

ᵃ24 Or *I am he*; also in verse 28

²⁵"Who are you?" they asked.

"Just what I have been claiming all along," Jesus replied. ²⁶"I have much to say in judgment of you. But he who sent me is reliable, and what I have heard from him I tell the world."

²⁷They did not understand that he was telling them about his Father. ²⁸So Jesus said, "When you have lifted up the Son of Man, then you will know that I am the one I claim to be, and that I do nothing on my own but speak just what the Father has taught me. ²⁹The one who sent me is with me; he has not left me alone, for I always do what pleases him." ³⁰Even as he spoke, many put their faith in him.

FREE FROM SIN

³¹**To the Jews who had believed him, Jesus said, "If you hold to my teaching, you are really my disciples. ³²Then you will know the truth, and the truth will set you free."**

³³They answered him, "We are Abraham's descendants*ᵃ* and have never been slaves of anyone. How can you say that we shall be set free?"

³⁴Jesus replied, "I tell you the truth, everyone who sins is a slave to sin. ³⁵Now a slave has no permanent place in the family, but a son belongs to it forever. ³⁶So if the Son sets you free, you will be free indeed. ³⁷I know you are Abraham's descendants. Yet you are ready to kill me, because

---

*ᵃ33 Greek *seed*; also in verse 37*

JOHN 8:31-32

True Freedom

TO THE JEWS who had recognized Him as the Messiah, Jesus said, "If you hold to my teaching, you are really my disciples. Then you will know the truth, and the truth will set you free."

Many people ask, "Where am I going? What is the answer to life? Do I have a purpose?" Our society has many answers, but those answers don't satisfy completely. The freeing truth that Jesus offers isn't political or intellectual—it's about a relationship with Him. *That* truth leads to freedom from sin and death.

Jesus' truth makes us free from religious rules, addictions, wrong things we have done, and harmful cycles in our lives. When we find a personal relationship with Jesus and follow His teachings, we find relief, release, and the way out. Knowing Jesus' true identity makes us truly free to serve God and fulfill His purpose for our lives. We find truth by knowing Jesus, who *is* the Truth.

you have no room for my word. [38]I am telling you what I have seen in the Father's presence, and you do what you have heard from your father.*[a]*"

[39]"Abraham is our father," they answered.

"If you were Abraham's children," said Jesus, "then you would*[b]* do the things Abraham did. [40]As it is, you are determined to kill me, a man who has told you the truth that I heard from God. Abraham did not do such things. [41]You are doing the things your own father does."

"We are not illegitimate children," they protested. "The only Father we have is God himself."

JESUS GIVES A STERN WARNING

[42]Jesus said to them, "If God were your Father, you would love me, for I came from God and now am here. I have not come on my own; but he sent me. [43]Why is my language not clear to you? Because you are unable to hear what I say. [44]You belong to your father, the devil, and you want to carry out your father's desire. He was a murderer from the beginning, not holding to the truth, for there is no truth in him. When he lies, he speaks his native language, for he is a liar and the father of lies. [45]Yet because I tell the truth, you do not believe me! [46]Can any of you prove me guilty of sin? If I am telling the truth, why don't you believe me? [47]He who belongs to God hears what God says. The reason you do not hear is that you do not belong to God."

"BEFORE ABRAHAM WAS BORN, I AM!" WHY WAS THIS STATEMENT SO SCANDALOUS?

By making this statement, Jesus was equating Himself to God, saying He had been around long before the Jews' ancient ancestor Abraham—in fact, He had been with God forever. Jesus' listeners considered this statement to be blasphemy (contempt of God). That's why they tried to kill Him. Many people try to say that Jesus was a great moral teacher, nothing more. Statements like this, however, show that Jesus claimed to be far more than just a Teacher. He claimed to be God.

JESUS' CLAIMS ABOUT HIMSELF

[48]The Jews answered him, "Aren't we right in saying that you are a Samaritan and demon-possessed?"

[49]"I am not possessed by a demon," said Jesus, "but I honor my Father and you dishonor me. [50]I am not seeking glory for myself; but there is one who seeks it, and he is the judge. [51]I tell you the truth, if anyone keeps my word, he will never see death."

[52]At this the Jews exclaimed, "Now we know that you are demon-possessed! Abraham died and so did the prophets, yet you say that if anyone keeps your word, he will never taste death. [53]Are you greater than our father Abraham? He died, and so did the prophets. Who do you think you are?"

[54]Jesus replied, "If I glorify myself, my glory means nothing. My Father, whom you claim as your God, is the one who glorifies me. [55]Though you do not know him, I know him. If I said I

---

*[a]*38 Or *presence. Therefore do what you have heard from the Father.*   *[b]*39 Some early manuscripts *"If you are Abraham's children," said Jesus, "then*

did not, I would be a liar like you, but I do know him and keep his word. 56Your father Abraham rejoiced at the thought of seeing my day; he saw it and was glad."

57"You are not yet fifty years old," the Jews said to him, "and you have seen Abraham!"

58"I tell you the truth," Jesus answered, "before Abraham was born, I am!" 59At this, they picked up stones to stone him, but Jesus hid himself, slipping away from the temple grounds.

JESUS HEALS A MAN BORN BLIND

9 As he went along, he saw a man blind from birth. 2His disciples asked him, "Rabbi, who sinned, this man or his parents, that he was born blind?"

3"Neither this man nor his parents sinned," said Jesus, "but this happened so that the work of God might be displayed in his life. 4As long as it is day, we must do the work of him who sent me. Night is coming, when no one can work. 5While I am in the world, I am the light of the world."

6Having said this, he spit on the ground, made some mud with the saliva, and put it on the man's eyes. 7"Go," he told him, "wash in the Pool of Siloam" (this word means Sent). So the man went and washed, and came home seeing.

WHOSE FAULT IS SUFFERING?

People wanted to know whose fault it was that the man in this story was born blind—was it his own fault, or his parents' fault, or something else? Jews believed sin caused suffering. Some people still want to assign blame when they see suffering. Jesus made the point that no one was at fault, and He proceeded to demonstrate God's power to work in this blind man's life by healing him.

8His neighbors and those who had formerly seen him begging asked, "Isn't this the same man who used to sit and beg?" 9Some claimed that he was.

Others said, "No, he only looks like him."

But he himself insisted, "I am the man."

10"How then were your eyes opened?" they demanded.

11He replied, "The man they call Jesus made some mud and put it on my eyes. He told me to go to Siloam and wash. So I went and washed, and then I could see."

12"Where is this man?" they asked him.

"I don't know," he said.

THE PHARISEES INVESTIGATE THE HEALING

13They brought to the Pharisees the man who had been blind. 14Now the day on which Jesus had made the mud and opened the man's eyes was a Sabbath. 15Therefore the Pharisees also asked him how he had received his sight. "He put mud on my eyes," the man replied, "and I washed, and now I see."

16Some of the Pharisees said, "This man is not from God, for he does not keep the Sabbath."

But others asked, "How can a sinner do such miraculous signs?" So they were divided.

¹⁷Finally they turned again to the blind man, "What have you to say about him? It was your eyes he opened."

The man replied, "He is a prophet."

¹⁸The Jews still did not believe that he had been blind and had received his sight until they sent for the man's parents. ¹⁹"Is this your son?" they asked. "Is this the one you say was born blind? How is it that now he can see?"

²⁰"We know he is our son," the parents answered, "and we know he was born blind. ²¹But how he can see now, or who opened his eyes, we don't know. Ask him. He is of age; he will speak for himself." ²²His parents said this because they were afraid of the Jews, for already the Jews had decided that anyone who acknowledged that Jesus was the Christ*ᵃ* would be put out of the synagogue. ²³That was why his parents said, "He is of age; ask him."

²⁴A second time they summoned the man who had been blind. "Give glory to God,*ᵇ*" they said. "We know this man is a sinner."

²⁵He replied, "Whether he is a sinner or not, I don't know. One thing I do know. I was blind but now I see!"

²⁶Then they asked him, "What did he do to you? How did he open your eyes?"

²⁷He answered, "I have told you already and you did not listen. Why do you want to hear it again? Do you want to become his disciples, too?"

²⁸Then they hurled insults at him and said, "You are this fellow's disciple! We are disciples of Moses! ²⁹We know that God spoke to Moses, but as for this fellow, we don't even know where he comes from."

³⁰The man answered, "Now that is remarkable! You don't know where he comes from, yet he opened my eyes. ³¹We know that God does not listen to sinners. He listens to the godly man who does his will. ³²Nobody has ever heard of opening the eyes of a man born blind. ³³If this man were not from God, he could do nothing."

³⁴To this they replied, "You were steeped in sin at birth; how dare you lecture us!" And they threw him out.

THE BLIND WILL SEE

³⁵Jesus heard that they had thrown him out, and when he found him, he said, "Do you believe in the Son of Man?"

³⁶"Who is he, sir?" the man asked. "Tell me so that I may believe in him."

³⁷Jesus said, "You have now seen him; in fact, he is the one speaking with you."

³⁸Then the man said, "Lord, I believe," and he worshiped him.

---

*ᵃ*22 Or *Messiah*   *ᵇ*24 A solemn charge to tell the truth (see Joshua 7:19)

³⁹Jesus said, "For judgment I have come into this world, so that the blind will see and those who see will become blind."

⁴⁰Some Pharisees who were with him heard him say this and asked, "What? Are we blind too?"

⁴¹Jesus said, "If you were blind, you would not be guilty of sin; but now that you claim you can see, your guilt remains.

THE SHEPHERD AND HIS FLOCK

10 "I tell you the truth, the man who does not enter the sheep pen by the gate, but climbs in by some other way, is a thief and a robber. ²The man who enters by the gate is the shepherd of his sheep. ³The watchman opens the gate for him, and the sheep listen to his voice. He calls his own sheep by name and leads them out. ⁴When he has brought out all his own, he goes on ahead of them, and his sheep follow him because they know his voice. ⁵But they will never follow a stranger; in fact, they will run away from him because they do not recognize a stranger's voice." ⁶Jesus used this figure of speech, but they did not understand what he was telling them.

⁷Therefore Jesus said again, "I tell you the truth, I am the gate for the sheep. ⁸All who ever came before me were thieves and robbers, but the sheep did not listen to them. ⁹I am the gate; whoever enters through me will be saved.ᵃ He will come in and go out, and find pasture. ¹⁰The thief comes only to steal and kill and destroy; I have come that they may have life, and have it to the full.

¹¹"I am the good shepherd. The good shepherd lays down his life for the sheep. ¹²The hired hand is not the shepherd who owns the sheep. So when he sees the wolf coming, he abandons the sheep and runs away. Then the wolf attacks the flock and scatters it. ¹³The man runs away because he is a hired hand and cares nothing for the sheep.

¹⁴"I am the good shepherd; I know my sheep and my sheep know me— ¹⁵just as the Father knows me and I know the Father— and I lay down my life for the sheep. ¹⁶I have other sheep that are not of this sheep pen. I must bring them also. They too will listen to my voice, and there shall be one flock and one shepherd. ¹⁷The reason my Father loves me is that I lay down my life—only to take it up again. ¹⁸No one takes it from me, but I lay it down of my own accord. I have authority to lay it down and authority to take it up again. This command I received from my Father."

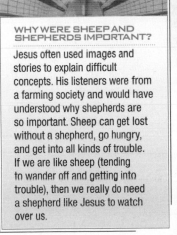

WHY WERE SHEEP AND SHEPHERDS IMPORTANT?

Jesus often used images and stories to explain difficult concepts. His listeners were from a farming society and would have understood why shepherds are so important. Sheep can get lost without a shepherd, go hungry, and get into all kinds of trouble. If we are like sheep (tending to wander off and getting into trouble), then we really do need a shepherd like Jesus to watch over us.

ᵃ9 Or *kept safe*

¹⁹At these words the Jews were again divided. ²⁰Many of them said, "He is demon-possessed and raving mad. Why listen to him?"

²¹But others said, "These are not the sayings of a man possessed by a demon. Can a demon open the eyes of the blind?"

THE UNBELIEF OF THE JEWS

²²Then came the Feast of Dedication^a at Jerusalem. It was winter, ²³and Jesus was in the temple area walking in Solomon's Colonnade. ²⁴The Jews gathered around him, saying, "How long will you keep us in suspense? If you are the Christ,^b tell us plainly."

²⁵Jesus answered, "I did tell you, but you do not believe. The miracles I do in my Father's name speak for me, ²⁶but you do not believe because you are not my sheep. ²⁷My sheep listen to my voice; I know them, and they follow me. ²⁸I give them eternal life, and they shall never perish; no one can snatch them out of my hand. ²⁹My Father, who has given them to me, is greater than all^c; no one can snatch them out of my Father's hand. ³⁰I and the Father are one."

³¹Again the Jews picked up stones to stone him, ³²but Jesus said to them, "I have shown you many great miracles from the Father. For which of these do you stone me?"

³³"We are not stoning you for any of these," replied the Jews, "but for blasphemy, because you, a mere man, claim to be God."

³⁴Jesus answered them, "Is it not written in your Law, 'I have said you are gods'^d? ³⁵If he called them 'gods,' to whom the word of God came— and the Scripture cannot be broken— ³⁶what about the one whom the Father set apart as his very own and sent into the world? Why then do you accuse me of blasphemy because I said, 'I am God's Son'? ³⁷Do not believe me unless I do what my Father does. ³⁸But if I do it, even though you do not believe me, believe the miracles, that you may know and understand that the Father is in me, and I in the Father." ³⁹Again they tried to seize him, but he escaped their grasp.

⁴⁰Then Jesus went back across the Jordan to the place where John had been baptizing in the early days. Here he stayed ⁴¹and many people came to him. They said, "Though John never performed a miraculous sign, all that John said about this man was true." ⁴²And in that place many believed in Jesus.

THE DEATH OF LAZARUS

11 Now a man named Lazarus was sick. He was from Bethany, the village of Mary and her sister Martha. ²This Mary, whose brother Lazarus now lay sick, was the same one who poured perfume on the Lord and wiped his feet with her hair. ³So the sisters sent word to Jesus, "Lord, the one you love is sick."

⁴When he heard this, Jesus said, "This sickness will not end in death.

---

^a22 That is, Hanukkah   ^b24 Or *Messiah*   ^c29 Many early manuscripts *What my Father has given me is greater than all*   ^d34 Psalm 82:6

No, it is for God's glory so that God's Son may be glorified through it." ⁵Jesus loved Martha and her sister and Lazarus. ⁶Yet when he heard that Lazarus was sick, he stayed where he was two more days.

⁷Then he said to his disciples, "Let us go back to Judea."

⁸"But Rabbi," they said, "a short while ago the Jews tried to stone you, and yet you are going back there?"

⁹Jesus answered, "Are there not twelve hours of daylight? A man who walks by day will not stumble, for he sees by this world's light. ¹⁰It is when he walks by night that he stumbles, for he has no light."

¹¹After he had said this, he went on to tell them, "Our friend Lazarus has fallen asleep; but I am going there to wake him up."

¹²His disciples replied, "Lord, if he sleeps, he will get better." ¹³Jesus had been speaking of his death, but his disciples thought he meant natural sleep.

¹⁴So then he told them plainly, "Lazarus is dead, ¹⁵and for your sake I am glad I was not there, so that you may believe. But let us go to him."

¹⁶Then Thomas (called Didymus) said to the rest of the disciples, "Let us also go, that we may die with him."

JESUS COMFORTS THE SISTERS

¹⁷On his arrival, Jesus found that Lazarus had already been in the tomb for four days. ¹⁸Bethany was less than two miles[a] from Jerusalem, ¹⁹and many Jews had come to Martha and Mary to comfort them in the loss of their brother. ²⁰When Martha heard that Jesus was coming, she went out to meet him, but Mary stayed at home.

²¹"Lord," Martha said to Jesus, "if you had been here, my brother would not have died. ²²But I know that even now God will give you whatever you ask."

²³Jesus said to her, "Your brother will rise again."

²⁴Martha answered, "I know he will rise again in the resurrection at the last day."

²⁵Jesus said to her, "I am the resurrection and the life. He who believes in me will live, even though he dies; ²⁶and whoever lives and believes in me will never die. Do you believe this?"

²⁷"Yes, Lord," she told him, "I believe that you are the Christ,[b] the Son of God, who was to come into the world."

²⁸And after she had said this, she went back and called her sister Mary aside. "The Teacher is here," she said, "and is asking for you." ²⁹When Mary heard this, she got up quickly and went to him. ³⁰Now Jesus had not yet entered the village, but was still at the place where Martha had met him. ³¹When the Jews who had been with Mary in the house, comforting her, noticed how quickly she got up and went out, they followed her, supposing she was going to the tomb to mourn there.

---

[a]18 Greek *fifteen stadia* (about 3 kilometers)   [b]27 Or *Messiah*

PEOPLE ATTEND THE Alpha course for many different reasons: some want to find answers, some are searching for fulfillment, some even come to prove that Christianity is false. Hamid became curious about the things his daughter was learning in church with her mother, so he began to look for answers about Christianity himself. He didn't really know where to start until a friend recommended the Alpha course. Hamid explains how he found answers to his questions, a community of friends, and the desire to become a Christian.

LOOKING FOR SOMETHING

HAMID'S STORY

I was born in Iran to parents who were Sufi Muslim. We were not really religious. When the revolution of 1979 happened, we were the religious minority. We had no freedom, so I escaped and came to the United States.

From the moment I set foot in this country, I was always looking for something, but I didn't know where to start or where to go. I was married to a Christian woman and my daughter, who is seven years old now, was baptized in a Christian church. However, our marriage didn't last and we got divorced. After my divorce, I was able to see my daughter only every other weekend. I knew that on the weekends that she wasn't with me, she was going to church. I wanted to make sure that she could also go to church on the weekends when she was with me. Even more, I began to be curious about the things my daughter believed, so I started looking for a place where I could learn the basics of Christianity. A friend recommended the Alpha course, and I contacted a church in my area where I could attend.

The first time I walked into the church, I was a bit worried. I didn't know anyone at the church and I didn't know what to expect. I was afraid they'd ask me a question about Christianity and I wouldn't know the answer. I had my guard up. I didn't want anyone to force me to believe something I didn't want to believe. I was just curious, that was it.

The first night of the Alpha course changed everything—I knew this was what I wanted. After the video, we broke up into small groups. We had eight people at our table. One of the guys had come to Alpha intending to show everyone else that Christianity and all of its claims were not true. Another guy came in thinking that he knew everything. The leader of the table led us in discussion. We could say whatever we wanted and no one was offended. We could ask whatever questions we had, and they took us seriously. We talked and laughed and had a wonderful evening. I knew I would come back. In fact, those two guys are now two of my closest friends. We continued to meet as a group throughout the course. We all were touched and changed in different ways.

It was so attractive to me that they let me go at my own pace. They were patient with my questions. By the time we went to the retreat, I decided, *If this is Christianity, then I want to be a Christian.* I started asking, "What do I do to become a Christian?" When I decided I wanted to do this, they were all there to help me; not once did anyone push me.

The moment I realized the power and importance of what had happened to me on the Alpha course was when I bought a yearbook from my daughter's school and asked her to sign it for me. She wrote: *Dad, thanks for taking me to church*, and I started crying.

WE COULD ASK WHATEVER QUESTIONS WE HAD, AND THEY TOOK US SERIOUSLY.

I love my daughter—there is nothing I would not do for her. Of all the stuff I have bought her, the thing that stays with her and impresses her the most is my taking her to church every other Sunday. Because of her, my life has changed. I am now a Christian.

³²When Mary reached the place where Jesus was and saw him, she fell at his feet and said, "Lord, if you had been here, my brother would not have died."

³³When Jesus saw her weeping, and the Jews who had come along with her also weeping, he was deeply moved in spirit and troubled. ³⁴"Where have you laid him?" he asked.

"Come and see, Lord," they replied.

³⁵Jesus wept.

³⁶Then the Jews said, "See how he loved him!"

³⁷But some of them said, "Could not he who opened the eyes of the blind man have kept this man from dying?"

JESUS RAISES LAZARUS FROM THE DEAD

³⁸Jesus, once more deeply moved, came to the tomb. It was a cave with a stone laid across the entrance. ³⁹"Take away the stone," he said.

"But, Lord," said Martha, the sister of the dead man, "by this time there is a bad odor, for he has been there four days."

⁴⁰Then Jesus said, "Did I not tell you that if you believed, you would see the glory of God?"

⁴¹So they took away the stone. Then Jesus looked up and said, "Father, I thank you that you have heard me. ⁴²I knew that you always hear me, but I said this for the benefit of the people standing here, that they may believe that you sent me."

⁴³When he had said this, Jesus called in a loud voice, "Lazarus, come out!" ⁴⁴The dead man came out, his hands and feet wrapped with strips of linen, and a cloth around his face.

Jesus said to them, "Take off the grave clothes and let him go."

THE PLOT TO KILL JESUS

⁴⁵Therefore many of the Jews who had come to visit Mary, and had seen what Jesus did, put their faith in him. ⁴⁶But some of them went to the Pharisees and told them what Jesus had done. ⁴⁷Then the chief priests and the Pharisees called a meeting of the Sanhedrin.

"What are we accomplishing?" they asked. "Here is this man performing many miraculous signs. ⁴⁸If we let him go on like this, everyone will believe in him, and then the Romans will come and take away both our place*ᵃ* and our nation."

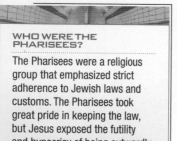

WHO WERE THE PHARISEES?

The Pharisees were a religious group that emphasized strict adherence to Jewish laws and customs. The Pharisees took great pride in keeping the law, but Jesus exposed the futility and hypocrisy of being outwardly "holy" while remaining inwardly sinful. He said that it is impossible for people to save themselves by keeping the law because no one is able to keep it perfectly. Other religious groups of the time, such as the Sadducees, are also mentioned in the Gospels. Each group had a different religious perspective, but all were offended by Jesus' words and actions.

---

*ᵃ*48 Or *temple*

⁴⁹Then one of them, named Caiaphas, who was high priest that year, spoke up, "You know nothing at all! ⁵⁰You do not realize that it is better for you that one man die for the people than that the whole nation perish."

⁵¹He did not say this on his own, but as high priest that year he prophesied that Jesus would die for the Jewish nation, ⁵²and not only for that nation but also for the scattered children of God, to bring them together and make them one. ⁵³So from that day on they plotted to take his life.

⁵⁴Therefore Jesus no longer moved about publicly among the Jews. Instead he withdrew to a region near the desert, to a village called Ephraim, where he stayed with his disciples.

⁵⁵When it was almost time for the Jewish Passover, many went up from the country to Jerusalem for their ceremonial cleansing before the Passover. ⁵⁶They kept looking for Jesus, and as they stood in the temple area they asked one another, "What do you think? Isn't he coming to the Feast at all?" ⁵⁷But the chief priests and Pharisees had given orders that if anyone found out where Jesus was, he should report it so that they might arrest him.

MARY WORSHIPS AT JESUS' FEET

12 Six days before the Passover, Jesus arrived at Bethany, where Lazarus lived, whom Jesus had raised from the dead. ²Here a dinner was given in Jesus' honor. Martha served, while Lazarus was among those reclining at the table with him. ³Then Mary took about a pint*ᵃ* of pure nard, an expensive perfume; she poured it on Jesus' feet and wiped his feet with her hair. And the house was filled with the fragrance of the perfume.

⁴But one of his disciples, Judas Iscariot, who was later to betray him, objected, ⁵"Why wasn't this perfume sold and the money given to the poor? It was worth a year's wages.*ᵇ*" ⁶He did not say this because he cared about the poor but because he was a thief; as keeper of the money bag, he used to help himself to what was put into it.

⁷"Leave her alone," Jesus replied. "⌐It was intended⌐ that she should save this perfume for the day of my burial. ⁸You will always have the poor among you, but you will not always have me."

⁹Meanwhile a large crowd of Jews found out that Jesus was there and came, not only because of him but also to see Lazarus, whom he had raised from the dead. ¹⁰So the chief priests made plans to kill Lazarus as well, ¹¹for on account of him many of the Jews were going over to Jesus and putting their faith in him.

A GRAND ENTRANCE

¹²The next day the great crowd that had come for the Feast heard that Jesus was on his way to Jerusalem. ¹³They took palm branches and went out to meet him, shouting,

---

*ᵃ*3 Greek *a litra* (probably about 0.5 liter)   *ᵇ*5 Greek *three hundred denarii*

"Hosanna!*ª*"

"Blessed is he who comes in the name of the Lord!"*ᵇ*

"Blessed is the King of Israel!"

¹⁴Jesus found a young donkey and sat upon it, as it is written,

¹⁵ "Do not be afraid, O Daughter of Zion;
   see, your king is coming,
   seated on a donkey's colt."*ᶜ*

¹⁶At first his disciples did not understand all this. Only after Jesus was glorified did they realize that these things had been written about him and that they had done these things to him. ¹⁷Now the crowd that was with him when he called Lazarus from the tomb and raised him from the dead continued to spread the word. ¹⁸Many people, because they had heard that he had given this miraculous sign, went out to meet him. ¹⁹So the Pharisees said to one another, "See, this is getting us nowhere. Look how the whole world has gone after him!"

JESUS PREDICTS HIS DEATH

²⁰Now there were some Greeks among those who went up to worship at the Feast. ²¹They came to Philip, who was from Bethsaida in Galilee, with a request. "Sir," they said, "we would like to see Jesus." ²²Philip went to tell Andrew; Andrew and Philip in turn told Jesus.

²³Jesus replied, "The hour has come for the Son of Man to be glorified. ²⁴I tell you the truth, unless a kernel of wheat falls to the ground and dies, it remains only a single seed. But if it dies, it produces many seeds. ²⁵The man who loves his life will lose it, while the man who hates his life in this world will keep it for eternal life. ²⁶Whoever serves me must follow me; and where I am, my servant also will be. My Father will honor the one who serves me.

²⁷"Now my heart is troubled, and what shall I say? 'Father, save me from this hour'? No, it was for this very reason I came to this hour. ²⁸Father, glorify your name!"

Then a voice came from heaven, "I have glorified it, and will glorify it again." ²⁹The crowd that was there and heard it said it had thundered; others said an angel had spoken to him.

³⁰Jesus said, "This voice was for your benefit, not mine. ³¹Now is the time for judgment on this world; now the prince of this world will be driven out. ³²But I, when I am lifted up from the earth, will draw all men to myself." ³³He said this to show the kind of death he was going to die.

³⁴The crowd spoke up, "We have heard from the Law that the Christ*ᵈ* will remain forever, so how can you say, 'The Son of Man must be lifted up'? Who is this 'Son of Man'?"

---

*ª*13 A Hebrew expression meaning "Save!" which became an exclamation of praise   *ᵇ*13 Psalm 118:25,26   *ᶜ*15 Zech. 9:9   *ᵈ*34 Or *Messiah*

35Then Jesus told them, "You are going to have the light just a little while longer. Walk while you have the light, before darkness overtakes you. The man who walks in the dark does not know where he is going. 36Put your trust in the light while you have it, so that you may become sons of light." When he had finished speaking, Jesus left and hid himself from them.

THE JEWS CONTINUE IN THEIR UNBELIEF

37Even after Jesus had done all these miraculous signs in their presence, they still would not believe in him. 38This was to fulfill the word of Isaiah the prophet:

"Lord, who has believed our message
and to whom has the arm of the Lord been revealed?"[a]

39For this reason they could not believe, because, as Isaiah says elsewhere:

40 "He has blinded their eyes
and deadened their hearts,
so they can neither see with their eyes,
nor understand with their hearts,
nor turn—and I would heal them."[b]

41Isaiah said this because he saw Jesus' glory and spoke about him.

42Yet at the same time many even among the leaders believed in him. But because of the Pharisees they would not confess their faith for fear they would be put out of the synagogue; 43for they loved praise from men more than praise from God.

44Then Jesus cried out, "When a man believes in me, he does not believe in me only, but in the one who sent me. 45When he looks at me, he sees the one who sent me. 46I have come into the world as a light, so that no one who believes in me should stay in darkness.

47"As for the person who hears my words but does not keep them, I do not judge him. For I did not come to judge the world, but to save it. 48There is a judge for the one who rejects me and does not accept my words; that very word which I spoke will condemn him at the last day. 49For I did not speak of my own accord, but the Father who sent me commanded me what to say and how to say it. 50I know that his command leads to eternal life. So whatever I say is just what the Father has told me to say."

JESUS WASHES HIS DISCIPLES' FEET

13 It was just before the Passover Feast. Jesus knew that the time had come for him to leave this world and go to the Father. Having loved his own who were in the world, he now showed them the full extent of his love.[c]

---

[a]38 Isaiah 53:1　[b]40 Isaiah 6:10　[c]1 Or *he loved them to the last*

²The evening meal was being served, and the devil had already prompted Judas Iscariot, son of Simon, to betray Jesus. ³Jesus knew that the Father had put all things under his power, and that he had come from God and was returning to God; ⁴so he got up from the meal, took off his outer clothing, and wrapped a towel around his waist. ⁵After that, he poured water into a basin and began to wash his disciples' feet, drying them with the towel that was wrapped around him.

⁶He came to Simon Peter, who said to him, "Lord, are you going to wash my feet?"

⁷Jesus replied, "You do not realize now what I am doing, but later you will understand."

⁸"No," said Peter, "you shall never wash my feet."

Jesus answered, "Unless I wash you, you have no part with me."

⁹"Then, Lord," Simon Peter replied, "not just my feet but my hands and my head as well!"

¹⁰Jesus answered, "A person who has had a bath needs only to wash his feet; his whole body is clean. And you are clean, though not every one of you." ¹¹For he knew who was going to betray him, and that was why he said not every one was clean.

WHY DID JESUS WASH THE DISCIPLES' FEET?

Ancient Palestine was a hot and dusty climate where people wore sandals and walked frequently. Because of this, it was a common act of hospitality to provide guests with water for washing their feet upon arrival. Those wealthy enough to have servants would dispatch a servant to perform this duty. When Jesus washed His disciples' feet, He took on the role of a servant, humbled Himself, and gave a powerful example of leadership. He wanted His disciples to understand that the pathway to greatness in His kingdom is not by self-assertion but through serving others.

¹²When he had finished washing their feet, he put on his clothes and returned to his place. "Do you understand what I have done for you?" he asked them. ¹³"You call me 'Teacher' and 'Lord,' and rightly so, for that is what I am. ¹⁴Now that I, your Lord and Teacher, have washed your feet, you also should wash one another's feet. ¹⁵I have set you an example that you should do as I have done for you. ¹⁶I tell you the truth, no servant is greater than his master, nor is a messenger greater than the one who sent him. ¹⁷Now that you know these things, you will be blessed if you do them.

JESUS PREDICTS HIS BETRAYAL

¹⁸"I am not referring to all of you; I know those I have chosen. But this is to fulfill the scripture: 'He who shares my bread has lifted up his heel against me.'[a]

¹⁹"I am telling you now before it happens, so that when it does happen you will believe that I am He. ²⁰I tell you the truth, whoever accepts any-

---

[a]18 Psalm 41:9

one I send accepts me; and whoever accepts me accepts the one who sent me."

²¹After he had said this, Jesus was troubled in spirit and testified, "I tell you the truth, one of you is going to betray me."

²²His disciples stared at one another, at a loss to know which of them he meant. ²³One of them, the disciple whom Jesus loved, was reclining next to him. ²⁴Simon Peter motioned to this disciple and said, "Ask him which one he means."

²⁵Leaning back against Jesus, he asked him, "Lord, who is it?"

²⁶Jesus answered, "It is the one to whom I will give this piece of bread when I have dipped it in the dish." Then, dipping the piece of bread, he gave it to Judas Iscariot, son of Simon. ²⁷As soon as Judas took the bread, Satan entered into him.

"What you are about to do, do quickly," Jesus told him, ²⁸but no one at the meal understood why Jesus said this to him. ²⁹Since Judas had charge of the money, some thought Jesus was telling him to buy what was needed for the Feast, or to give something to the poor. ³⁰As soon as Judas had taken the bread, he went out. And it was night.

JESUS PREDICTS PETER'S DENIAL

³¹When he was gone, Jesus said, "Now is the Son of Man glorified and God is glorified in him. ³²If God is glorified in him,ᵃ God will glorify the Son in himself, and will glorify him at once.

³³"My children, I will be with you only a little longer. You will look for me, and just as I told the Jews, so I tell you now: Where I am going, you cannot come.

³⁴"A new command I give you: Love one another. As I have loved you, so you must love one another. ³⁵By this all men will know that you are my disciples, if you love one another."

³⁶Simon Peter asked him, "Lord, where are you going?"

Jesus replied, "Where I am going, you cannot follow now, but you will follow later."

³⁷Peter asked, "Lord, why can't I follow you now? I will lay down my life for you."

³⁸Then Jesus answered, "Will you really lay down your life for me? I tell you the truth, before the rooster crows, you will disown me three times!

JESUS COMFORTS HIS DISCIPLES

14 "Do not let your hearts be troubled. Trust in God^b; trust also in me. ²In my Father's house are many rooms; if it were not so, I would have told you. I am going there to prepare a place for you. ³And if I go and prepare a place for you, I will come back and take you to be with me that you also may be where I am. ⁴You know the way to the place where I am going."

ᵃ32 Many early manuscripts do not have *If God is glorified in him.*   ᵇ1 Or *You trust in God*

JESUS IS THE WAY TO THE FATHER

⁵Thomas said to him, "Lord, we don't know where you are going, so how can we know the way?"

⁶Jesus answered, "I am the way and the truth and the life. No one comes to the Father except through me. ⁷If you really knew me, you would know*ᵃ* my Father as well. From now on, you do know him and have seen him."

⁸Philip said, "Lord, show us the Father and that will be enough for us."

⁹Jesus answered: "Don't you know me, Philip, even after I have been among you such a long time? Anyone who has seen me has seen the Father. How can you say, 'Show us the Father'? ¹⁰Don't you believe that I am in the Father, and that the Father is in me? The words I say to you are not just my own. Rather, it is the Father, living in me, who is doing his work. ¹¹Believe me when I say that I am in the Father and the Father is in me; or at least believe on the evidence of the miracles themselves. ¹²I tell you the truth, anyone who has faith in me will do what I have been doing. He will do even greater things than these, because I am going to the Father. ¹³And I will do whatever you ask in my name, so that the Son may bring glory to the Father. ¹⁴You may ask me for anything in my name, and I will do it.

JESUS PROMISES TO SEND THE HOLY SPIRIT

¹⁵"If you love me, you will obey what I command. ¹⁶And I will ask the Father, and he will give you another Counselor to be with you forever— ¹⁷the Spirit of truth. The world cannot accept him, because it neither sees him nor knows him. But you know him, for he lives with you and will be*ᵇ* in you. ¹⁸I will not leave you as orphans; I will come to you. ¹⁹Before long, the world will not see me anymore, but you will see me. Because I live, you also will live. ²⁰On that day you will realize that I am in my Father, and you are in me, and I am in you. ²¹Whoever has my commands and obeys them, he is the one who loves me. He who loves me will be loved by my Father, and I too will love him and show myself to him."

²²Then Judas (not Judas Iscariot) said, "But, Lord, why do you intend to show yourself to us and not to the world?"

²³Jesus replied, "If anyone loves me, he will obey my teaching. My Father will love him, and we will come to him and make our home with him. ²⁴He who does not love me will not obey my teaching. These words you hear are not my own; they belong to the Father who sent me.

²⁵"All this I have spoken while still with you. ²⁶**But the Counselor, the Holy Spirit, whom the Father will send in my name, will teach you all things and will remind you of everything I have said to you.** ²⁷Peace I leave with you; my peace I give you. I do not give to you as the world gives. Do not let your hearts be troubled and do not be afraid.

---

*ᵃ*7 Some early manuscripts *If you really have known me, you will know*   *ᵇ*17 Some early manuscripts *and is*

28"You heard me say, 'I am going away and I am coming back to you.' If you loved me, you would be glad that I am going to the Father, for the Father is greater than I. 29I have told you now before it happens, so that when it does happen you will believe. 30I will not speak with you much longer, for the prince of this world is coming. He has no hold on me, 31but the world must learn that I love the Father and that I do exactly what my Father has commanded me.

"Come now; let us leave.

A PICTURE OF OUR RELATIONSHIP WITH JESUS

15 "I am the true vine, and my Father is the gardener. 2He cuts off every branch in me that bears no fruit, while every branch that does bear fruit he prunes*a* so that it will be even more fruitful. 3You are already clean because of the word I have spoken to you. 4Remain in me, and I will remain in you. No branch can bear fruit by itself; it must remain in the vine. Neither can you bear fruit unless you remain in me.

5"I am the vine; you are the branches. If a man remains in me and I in him, he will bear much fruit; apart from me you can do nothing. 6If anyone does not remain in me, he is like a branch that is thrown away and withers; such branches are picked up, thrown into the fire and burned. 7If you remain in me and my words remain in you, ask whatever you wish,

---

*a*2 The Greek for *prunes* also means *cleans*.

JOHN 14:26

The Role of the Holy Spirit

BEFORE JESUS ASCENDED back to heaven, He made a promise to His followers: "The Counselor, the Holy Spirit, whom the Father will send in my name, will teach you all things and will remind you of everything I have said to you." In essence, He was saying that after He was gone from them physically, the Holy Spirit would come from God in His name and continue His ministry of teaching. Jesus, when on earth, could only be with a finite number of people at one time. But through the Spirit, He can be with all believers at once. The Holy Spirit came to remind the disciples of Jesus' teachings and helped them to accurately write the Gospels (the first four books of the New Testament). The Holy Spirit's continued teaching and reminding work also helped the other writers of the New Testament.

We can pray and ask the Holy Spirit (God Himself) to help us understand the Bible and remind us of God's words on a daily basis. As we study, memorize, and meditate on Christ's words, the Holy Spirit will help us apply them to our lives.

and it will be given you. [8]This is to my Father's glory, that you bear much fruit, showing yourselves to be my disciples.

[9]"As the Father has loved me, so have I loved you. Now remain in my love. [10]If you obey my commands, you will remain in my love, just as I have obeyed my Father's commands and remain in his love. [11]I have told you this so that my joy may be in you and that your joy may be complete. [12]My command is this: Love each other as I have loved you. [13]Greater love has no one than this, that he lay down his life for his friends. [14]You are my friends if you do what I command. [15]I no longer call you servants, because a servant does not know his master's business. Instead, I have called you friends, for everything that I learned from my Father I have made known to you. [16]You did not choose me, but I chose you and appointed you to go and bear fruit—fruit that will last. Then the Father will give you whatever you ask in my name. [17]This is my command: Love each other.

THE WORLD HATES THE DISCIPLES

[18]"If the world hates you, keep in mind that it hated me first. [19]If you belonged to the world, it would love you as its own. As it is, you do not belong to the world, but I have chosen you out of the world. That is why the world hates you. [20]Remember the words I spoke to you: 'No servant is greater than his master.'[a] If they persecuted me, they will persecute you also. If they obeyed my teaching, they will obey yours also. [21]They will treat you this way because of my name, for they do not know the One who sent me. [22]If I had not come and spoken to them, they would not be guilty of sin. Now, however, they have no excuse for their sin. [23]He who hates me hates my Father as well. [24]If I had not done among them what no one else did, they would not be guilty of sin. But now they have seen these miracles, and yet they have hated both me and my Father. [25]But this is to fulfill what is written in their Law: 'They hated me without reason.'[b]

[26]"When the Counselor comes, whom I will send to you from the Father, the Spirit of truth who goes out from the Father, he will testify about me. [27]And you also must testify, for you have been with me from the beginning.

16 "All this I have told you so that you will not go astray. [2]They will put you out of the synagogue; in fact, a time is coming when anyone who kills you will think he is offering a service to God. [3]They will do such things because they have not known the Father or me. [4]I have told you this, so that when the time comes you will remember that I warned you. I did not tell you this at first because I was with you.

THE WORK OF THE HOLY SPIRIT

[5]"Now I am going to him who sent me, yet none of you asks me, 'Where are you going?' [6]Because I have said these things, you are filled with grief. [7]But I tell you the truth: It is for your good that I am going away. Unless I go away, the Counselor will not come to you; but if I go, I will send him

---

[a]20 John 13:16 [b]25 Psalms 35:19; 69:4

to you. ⁸When he comes, he will convict the world of guilt*a* in regard to sin and righteousness and judgment: ⁹in regard to sin, because men do not believe in me; ¹⁰in regard to righteousness, because I am going to the Father, where you can see me no longer; ¹¹and in regard to judgment, because the prince of this world now stands condemned.

¹²"I have much more to say to you, more than you can now bear. **¹³But when he, the Spirit of truth, comes, he will guide you into all truth. He will not speak on his own; he will speak only what he hears, and he will tell you what is yet to come.** ¹⁴He will bring glory to me by taking from what is mine and making it known to you. ¹⁵All that belongs to the Father is mine. That is why I said the Spirit will take from what is mine and make it known to you.

¹⁶"In a little while you will see me no more, and then after a little while you will see me."

THE DISCIPLES' GRIEF WILL TURN TO JOY

¹⁷Some of his disciples said to one another, "What does he mean by saying, 'In a little while you will see me no more, and then after a little while you will see me,' and 'Because I am going to the Father'?" ¹⁸They kept asking, "What does he mean by 'a little while'? We don't understand what he is saying."

*a*8 Or *will expose the guilt of the world*

JOHN 16:13

Always with Us

THE NIGHT BEFORE He was crucified, Jesus spent extended time with His followers, giving them His last words. He spoke to them of what would come: His crucifixion, resurrection, and ascension (return to heaven). At this point, the disciples could not fully understand everything Jesus was talking about—they didn't believe Jesus was really going to die and couldn't comprehend His words about leaving them, the coming of the Holy Spirit, and their future mission. Jesus calmed them by explaining that "when he, the Spirit of truth, comes, he will guide you into all truth. He will not speak on his own; he will speak only what he hears, and he will tell you what is yet to come." The Holy Spirit would help them understand what to do and bring insight and clarification to Jesus' words.

The Holy Spirit is our teacher and guide as well. Jesus is no longer in human form on this earth, but His teaching ministry continues through the work of the Spirit, and He leads us in our daily decisions and actions.

¹⁹Jesus saw that they wanted to ask him about this, so he said to them, "Are you asking one another what I meant when I said, 'In a little while you will see me no more, and then after a little while you will see me'? ²⁰I tell you the truth, you will weep and mourn while the world rejoices. You will grieve, but your grief will turn to joy. ²¹A woman giving birth to a child has pain because her time has come; but when her baby is born she forgets the anguish because of her joy that a child is born into the world. ²²So with you: Now is your time of grief, but I will see you again and you will rejoice, and no one will take away your joy. ²³In that day you will no longer ask me anything. I tell you the truth, my Father will give you whatever you ask in my name. ²⁴Until now you have not asked for anything in my name. Ask and you will receive, and your joy will be complete.

²⁵"Though I have been speaking figuratively, a time is coming when I will no longer use this kind of language but will tell you plainly about my Father. ²⁶In that day you will ask in my name. I am not saying that I will ask the Father on your behalf. ²⁷No, the Father himself loves you because you have loved me and have believed that I came from God. ²⁸I came from the Father and entered the world; now I am leaving the world and going back to the Father."

²⁹Then Jesus' disciples said, "Now you are speaking clearly and without figures of speech. ³⁰Now we can see that you know all things and that you do not even need to have anyone ask you questions. This makes us believe that you came from God."

³¹"You believe at last!"ᵃ Jesus answered. ³²"But a time is coming, and has come, when you will be scattered, each to his own home. You will leave me all alone. Yet I am not alone, for my Father is with me.

³³"I have told you these things, so that in me you may have peace. In this world you will have trouble. But take heart! I have overcome the world."

JESUS PRAYS FOR HIMSELF

17 After Jesus said this, he looked toward heaven and prayed:

"Father, the time has come. Glorify your Son, that your Son may glorify you. ²For you granted him authority over all people that he might give eternal life to all those you have given him. ³Now this is eternal life: that they may know you, the only true God, and Jesus Christ, whom you have sent. ⁴I have brought you glory on earth by completing the work you gave me to do. ⁵And now, Father, glorify me in your presence with the glory I had with you before the world began.

JESUS PRAYS FOR HIS DISCIPLES

⁶"I have revealed youᵇ to those whom you gave me out of the world. They were yours; you gave them to me and they have obeyed your word. ⁷Now they know that everything you have given me comes

---

ᵃ31 Or "Do you now believe?"   ᵇ6 Greek your name; also in verse 26 from you. 8For I gave them the words you gave me and they accepted them. They knew with certainty that I came from you, and they believed that you sent me. 9I pray for them. I am not praying for the world, but for those you have given me, for they are yours. 10All I have is yours, and all you have is mine. And glory has come to me through them. 11I will remain in the world no longer, but they are still in the world, and I am coming to you. Holy Father, protect them by the power of your name—the name you gave me—so that they may be one as we are one. 12While I was with them, I protected them and kept them safe by that name you gave me. None has been lost except the one doomed to destruction so that Scripture would be fulfilled.

13"I am coming to you now, but I say these things while I am still in the world, so that they may have the full measure of my joy within them. 14**I have given them your word and the world has hated them, for they are not of the world any more than I am of the world.**

JOHN 17:14, 17

New Life

AFTER JESUS FINISHED speaking with His disciples, He went off alone to pray. He talked to God the Father, knowing that He was leaving the entire message of the Good News in the hands of a few followers who, even at this point, didn't completely understand it. He knew danger would come; He knew they would be hated for their faith. He prayed, "I have given them your word and the world has hated them, for they are not of the world any more than I am of the world." He asked that God would "sanctify them by the truth" (set them apart, free from sin).

These verses explain why Christians are different from the society around them. Those who come to believe in Jesus see life through God's eyes and have a new set of values. These values are often contrary to what the world believes and how it lives. God's Word and values expose the emptiness of the world's values, so the world often hates Christians and what they stand for.

When Jesus' words are properly understood and followed, they are not popular. The world tells us to serve ourselves; the Bible tells us to serve others. The world seeks revenge; Jesus teaches love and forgiveness. Christians are not "of the world" in the same way that Jesus was not. Christ's followers get their directions from God through the Bible, and they are sanctified (cleansed and purified) by the truth found in God's Word.

¹⁵My prayer is not that you take them out of the world but that you protect them from the evil one. ¹⁶They are not of the world, even as I am not of it. ¹⁷**Sanctify**ᵃ **them by the truth; your word is truth.** ¹⁸As you sent me into the world, I have sent them into the world. ¹⁹For them I sanctify myself, that they too may be truly sanctified.

JESUS PRAYS FOR ALL BELIEVERS

²⁰"My prayer is not for them alone. I pray also for those who will believe in me through their message, ²¹that all of them may be one, Father, just as you are in me and I am in you. May they also be in us so that the world may believe that you have sent me. ²²I have given them the glory that you gave me, that they may be one as we are one: ²³I in them and you in me. May they be brought to complete unity to let the world know that you sent me and have loved them even as you have loved me.

²⁴"Father, I want those you have given me to be with me where I am, and to see my glory, the glory you have given me because you loved me before the creation of the world.

²⁵"Righteous Father, though the world does not know you, I know you, and they know that you have sent me. ²⁶I have made you known to them, and will continue to make you known in order that the love you have for me may be in them and that I myself may be in them."

> **WHO DID JESUS PRAY FOR?**
>
> Before His arrest, Jesus prayed for Himself, His disciples, and then for all believers. He prayed for "those who will believe in me through their [the disciples'] message." That's you. You have heard the message because the disciples faithfully told it to people who told it to others and so on down through the centuries. Jesus prayed for *you!*

JESUS IS ARRESTED

18 When he had finished praying, Jesus left with his disciples and crossed the Kidron Valley. On the other side there was an olive grove, and he and his disciples went into it.

²Now Judas, who betrayed him, knew the place, because Jesus had often met there with his disciples. ³So Judas came to the grove, guiding a detachment of soldiers and some officials from the chief priests and Pharisees. They were carrying torches, lanterns and weapons.

⁴Jesus, knowing all that was going to happen to him, went out and asked them, "Who is it you want?"

⁵"Jesus of Nazareth," they replied.

"I am he," Jesus said. (And Judas the traitor was standing there with them.) ⁶When Jesus said, "I am he," they drew back and fell to the ground.

⁷Again he asked them, "Who is it you want?"

And they said, "Jesus of Nazareth."

ᵃ17 Greek *hagiazo* (*set apart for sacred use* or *make holy*); also in verse 19

8"I told you that I am he," Jesus answered. "If you are looking for me, then let these men go." 9This happened so that the words he had spoken would be fulfilled: "I have not lost one of those you gave me."[a]

10Then Simon Peter, who had a sword, drew it and struck the high priest's servant, cutting off his right ear. (The servant's name was Malchus.)

11Jesus commanded Peter, "Put your sword away! Shall I not drink the cup the Father has given me?"

JESUS IS TAKEN TO ANNAS

12Then the detachment of soldiers with its commander and the Jewish officials arrested Jesus. They bound him 13and brought him first to Annas, who was the father-in-law of Caiaphas, the high priest that year. 14Caiaphas was the one who had advised the Jews that it would be good if one man died for the people.

PETER CLAIMS TO NOT KNOW JESUS

15Simon Peter and another disciple were following Jesus. Because this disciple was known to the high priest, he went with Jesus into the high priest's courtyard, 16but Peter had to wait outside at the door. The other disciple, who was known to the high priest, came back, spoke to the girl on duty there and brought Peter in.

17"You are not one of his disciples, are you?" the girl at the door asked Peter.

He replied, "I am not."

18It was cold, and the servants and officials stood around a fire they had made to keep warm. Peter also was standing with them, warming himself.

THE HIGH PRIEST QUESTIONS JESUS

19Meanwhile, the high priest questioned Jesus about his disciples and his teaching.

20"I have spoken openly to the world," Jesus replied. "I always taught in synagogues or at the temple, where all the Jews come together. I said nothing in secret. 21Why question me? Ask those who heard me. Surely they know what I said."

22When Jesus said this, one of the officials nearby struck him in the face. "Is this the way you answer the high priest?" he demanded.

WHO WERE THESE AUTHORITIES WHO QUESTIONED JESUS?

After Jesus was arrested by the Jewish priests and officials, he was brought before several authorities for sentencing. Annas and Caiaphas were Jewish high priests who wanted Jesus to die because of His claims to be God. They did not have the ultimate authority to execute a prisoner in Roman territory, however, so they brought Jesus to Pontius Pilate (18:28–29), the local Roman governor. Pilate was reluctant, but ultimately the chief priests convinced him to free another prisoner and sanction Jesus' death.

[a]9 John 6:39

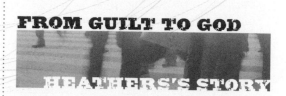

LIVING A LIFE of faith means different things for people who have been raised in different religious backgrounds. It can be difficult to take the Gospels for what they are and apply them to a life that isn't consistent with the Christian faith. It's important to remember that conversion begins in the heart and is a process that leads to salvation. This knowledge of salvation is not only life changing, but also peace giving and full of unconditional love. Heather was able to release her guilt and let God do the changing work in her heart.

FROM GUILT TO GOD

HEATHER'S STORY

I was raised Jewish and took it very seriously, although I had many questions about where we go when we die and who God is. I was the first girl in my family to have a Bat Mitzvah (an initiatory ceremony recognizing a Jewish girl as a daughter of the divine law), and I insisted on it.

If anybody talked to me about Jesus Christ I was offended. If ever I heard that a Jewish friend had read the New Testament, I was mortified.

But things started to change. One of my half-brothers converted to Christianity, so I tried reading the New Testament, but I didn't understand it.

When I moved away from home I stopped going to synagogue. I became very engrossed with my job in the fashion industry.

Friends who were opening a restaurant outside Chicago asked me to help with being a waitress part-time. In my first week a man walked in, and I told my friends, "That's the man I am going to marry." Gary was forty-five and divorced with three children. There was a seventeen-year age difference between us. And he was also a churchgoer.

A year and a half later, we married at a Christian and Jewish service. For the first year, Gary and I went to the synagogue on the high holidays. As a Jew, I felt that I should be there, and I wanted my husband to experience it with me. But I realized how far I'd drifted from Judaism. I didn't want to belong to a religion simply because it was a cultural process. So Gary and I decided to go to a friendly church where we could explore Christianity.

Still, I felt guilty that I wasn't going to the synagogue. At the same time, I was obsessed with religion: I read book after book—about Buddhism, Islam, the New Age, tarot cards, horoscopes.

One December, a nearby church put up an "Alpha Is Here!" sign. I had no idea what Alpha was. On Christmas Eve we went to the church and talked with a woman about the Alpha course. She said to come one night, listen, and see what we thought. So we went. And I loved every second of it. Our discussion group was boisterous and loud, with people from all different backgrounds. Everybody was involved.

I remember explaining to the group that comprehending the New Testament was like learning the sky was purple when I had known my whole life that it was blue. At night, I'd get into bed with my Bible and read something. I even asked God to make it okay for me to become a Christian because I was afraid of disappointing my parents.

IN THE MIDDLE OF OUR GROUP DISCUSSION I SAID, "I HAVE AN ANNOUNCEMENT TO MAKE . . ."

After the Alpha talk on "Does God Heal Today?" I had a long conversation with God: *I am sorry. I want to be forgiven for my sins. And I want to give my life to Christ. Show me now how You can use me.*

The following week I went back to the Alpha group, and in the middle of our group discussion I said, "I have an announcement to make . . ."

Kathleen, our leader, started crying. Gary was crying too.

Gary and I try to go to church every Sunday now. For Gary, Alpha was a spiritual workout. It helped him get his spiritual muscles back. And I've felt a weight lifted from my shoulders. I know that Jesus died for me, and I feel unconditionally loved.

My prayer used to be, *God, why won't You help me with this?* But now, I ask God what I can do for Him in order to thank Him for saving me. He's in charge of my life now. He gives me the tools and I get to be the vessel.

²³"If I said something wrong," Jesus replied, "testify as to what is wrong. But if I spoke the truth, why did you strike me?" ²⁴Then Annas sent him, still bound, to Caiaphas the high priest.ᵃ

PETER LIES A SECOND AND THIRD TIME

²⁵As Simon Peter stood warming himself, he was asked, "You are not one of his disciples, are you?"

He denied it, saying, "I am not."

²⁶One of the high priest's servants, a relative of the man whose ear Peter had cut off, challenged him, "Didn't I see you with him in the olive grove?" ²⁷Again Peter denied it, and at that moment a rooster began to crow.

PILATE QUESTIONS JESUS

²⁸Then the Jews led Jesus from Caiaphas to the palace of the Roman governor. By now it was early morning, and to avoid ceremonial uncleanness the Jews did not enter the palace; they wanted to be able to eat the Passover. ²⁹So Pilate came out to them and asked, "What charges are you bringing against this man?"

³⁰"If he were not a criminal," they replied, "we would not have handed him over to you."

³¹Pilate said, "Take him yourselves and judge him by your own law."

"But we have no right to execute anyone," the Jews objected. ³²This happened so that the words Jesus had spoken indicating the kind of death he was going to die would be fulfilled.

³³Pilate then went back inside the palace, summoned Jesus and asked him, "Are you the king of the Jews?"

³⁴"Is that your own idea," Jesus asked, "or did others talk to you about me?"

³⁵"Am I a Jew?" Pilate replied. "It was your people and your chief priests who handed you over to me. What is it you have done?"

³⁶Jesus said, "My kingdom is not of this world. If it were, my servants would fight to prevent my arrest by the Jews. But now my kingdom is from another place."

³⁷"You are a king, then!" said Pilate.

Jesus answered, "You are right in saying I am a king. In fact, for this reason I was born, and for this I came into the world, to testify to the truth. Everyone on the side of truth listens to me."

³⁸"What is truth?" Pilate asked. With this he went out again to the Jews and said, "I find no basis for a charge against him. ³⁹But it is your custom for me to release to you one prisoner at the time of the Passover. Do you want me to release 'the king of the Jews'?"

⁴⁰They shouted back, "No, not him! Give us Barabbas!" Now Barabbas had taken part in a rebellion.

ᵃ24 Or (*Now Annas had sent him, still bound, to Caiaphas the high priest.*)

JESUS IS SENTENCED TO DIE

19 Then Pilate took Jesus and had him flogged. [2]The soldiers twisted together a crown of thorns and put it on his head. They clothed him in a purple robe [3]and went up to him again and again, saying, "Hail, king of the Jews!" And they struck him in the face.

[4]Once more Pilate came out and said to the Jews, "Look, I am bringing him out to you to let you know that I find no basis for a charge against him." [5]When Jesus came out wearing the crown of thorns and the purple robe, Pilate said to them, "Here is the man!"

[6]As soon as the chief priests and their officials saw him, they shouted, "Crucify! Crucify!"

But Pilate answered, "You take him and crucify him. As for me, I find no basis for a charge against him."

[7]The Jews insisted, "We have a law, and according to that law he must die, because he claimed to be the Son of God."

[8]When Pilate heard this, he was even more afraid, [9]and he went back inside the palace. "Where do you come from?" he asked Jesus, but Jesus gave him no answer. [10]"Do you refuse to speak to me?" Pilate said. "Don't you realize I have power either to free you or to crucify you?"

[11]Jesus answered, "You would have no power over me if it were not given to you from above. Therefore the one who handed me over to you is guilty of a greater sin."

[12]From then on, Pilate tried to set Jesus free, but the Jews kept shouting, "If you let this man go, you are no friend of Caesar. Anyone who claims to be a king opposes Caesar."

[13]When Pilate heard this, he brought Jesus out and sat down on the judge's seat at a place known as the Stone Pavement (which in Aramaic is Gabbatha). [14]It was the day of Preparation of Passover Week, about the sixth hour.

"Here is your king," Pilate said to the Jews.

[15]But they shouted, "Take him away! Take him away! Crucify him!"

"Shall I crucify your king?" Pilate asked.

"We have no king but Caesar," the chief priests answered.

[16]Finally Pilate handed him over to them to be crucified.

JESUS IS NAILED TO A CROSS

So the soldiers took charge of Jesus. [17]Carrying his own cross, he went out to the place of the Skull (which in Aramaic is called Golgotha). [18]Here they crucified him, and with him two others—one on each side and Jesus in the middle.

[19]Pilate had a notice prepared and fastened to the cross. It read: JESUS OF NAZARETH, THE KING OF THE JEWS. [20]Many of the Jews read this sign, for the place where Jesus was crucified was near the city, and the sign was written in Aramaic, Latin and Greek. [21]The chief priests of the Jews

protested to Pilate, "Do not write 'The King of the Jews,' but that this man claimed to be king of the Jews."

[22]Pilate answered, "What I have written, I have written."

[23]When the soldiers crucified Jesus, they took his clothes, dividing them into four shares, one for each of them, with the undergarment remaining. This garment was seamless, woven in one piece from top to bottom.

[24]"Let's not tear it," they said to one another. "Let's decide by lot who will get it."

This happened that the scripture might be fulfilled which said,

> "They divided my garments among them
>   and cast lots for my clothing."[a]

So this is what the soldiers did.

[25]Near the cross of Jesus stood his mother, his mother's sister, Mary the wife of Clopas, and Mary Magdalene. [26]When Jesus saw his mother there, and the disciple whom he loved standing nearby, he said to his mother, "Dear woman, here is your son," [27]and to the disciple, "Here is your mother." From that time on, this disciple took her into his home.

WHY WAS JESUS PUT ON A CROSS?

Crucifixion, hanging on a cross, was a torturous and humiliating method of capital punishment used in the ancient world. This method of execution was considered extremely dishonorable and was reserved for slaves, the lowest of criminals, and traitors to the Roman empire. For an innocent Jesus to die on a cross was the ultimate in degradation—an overwhelming demonstration of love and sacrifice on behalf of others.

JESUS DIES

[28]Later, knowing that all was now completed, and so that the Scripture would be fulfilled, Jesus said, "I am thirsty." [29]A jar of wine vinegar was there, so they soaked a sponge in it, put the sponge on a stalk of the hyssop plant, and lifted it to Jesus' lips. [30]When he had received the drink, Jesus said, "It is finished." With that, he bowed his head and gave up his spirit.

[31]Now it was the day of Preparation, and the next day was to be a special Sabbath. Because the Jews did not want the bodies left on the crosses during the Sabbath, they asked Pilate to have the legs broken and the bodies taken down. [32]The soldiers therefore came and broke the legs of the first man who had been crucified with Jesus, and then those of the other. [33]But when they came to Jesus and found that he was already dead, they did not break his legs. [34]Instead, one of the soldiers pierced Jesus' side with a spear, bringing a sudden flow of blood and water. [35]The man who saw it has given testimony, and his testimony is true. He knows that he tells the truth, and he testifies so that you also may believe. [36]These things happened so that the scripture would be fulfilled: "Not one of his bones will be broken,"[b] [37]and, as another scripture says, "They will look on the one they have pierced."[c]

---

[a]24 Psalm 22:18   [b]36 Exodus 12:46; Num. 9:12; Psalm 34:20   [c]37 Zech. 12:10

JESUS IS BURIED

[38]Later, Joseph of Arimathea asked Pilate for the body of Jesus. Now Joseph was a disciple of Jesus, but secretly because he feared the Jews. With Pilate's permission, he came and took the body away. [39]He was accompanied by Nicodemus, the man who earlier had visited Jesus at night. Nicodemus brought a mixture of myrrh and aloes, about seventy-five pounds.[a] [40]Taking Jesus' body, the two of them wrapped it, with the spices, in strips of linen. This was in accordance with Jewish burial customs. [41]At the place where Jesus was crucified, there was a garden, and in the garden a new tomb, in which no one had ever been laid. [42]Because it was the Jewish day of Preparation and since the tomb was nearby, they laid Jesus there.

THE EMPTY TOMB

20 Early on the first day of the week, while it was still dark, Mary Magdalene went to the tomb and saw that the stone had been removed from the entrance. [2]So she came running to Simon Peter and the other disciple, the one Jesus loved, and said, "They have taken the Lord out of the tomb, and we don't know where they have put him!"

[3]So Peter and the other disciple started for the tomb. [4]Both were running, but the other disciple outran Peter and reached the tomb first. [5]He bent over and looked in at the strips of linen lying there but did not go in. [6]Then Simon Peter, who was behind him, arrived and went into the tomb. He saw the strips of linen lying there, [7]as well as the burial cloth that had been around Jesus' head. The cloth was folded up by itself, separate from the linen. [8]Finally the other disciple, who had reached the tomb first, also went inside. He saw and believed. [9](They still did not understand from Scripture that Jesus had to rise from the dead.)

JESUS APPEARS TO MARY MAGDALENE

[10]Then the disciples went back to their homes, [11]but Mary stood outside the tomb crying. As she wept, she bent over to look into the tomb [12]and saw two angels in white, seated where Jesus' body had been, one at the head and the other at the foot.

[13]They asked her, "Woman, why are you crying?"

"They have taken my Lord away," she said, "and I don't know where they have put him." [14]At this, she turned around and saw Jesus standing there, but she did not realize that it was Jesus.

IS THIS THE SAME NICODEMUS WHO WAS MENTIONED IN JOHN 3?

This was indeed the same man to whom Jesus spoke about being "born again." Earlier, Nicodemus had come at night because he hadn't wanted to admit his curiosity about Jesus. Here, he boldly helped Joseph of Arimathea prepare Jesus' body for burial. Nicodemus and Joseph were both members of the Sanhedrin, the council of Jewish leaders that had condemned Jesus to death. In doing this act of caring for and burying Jesus' body, they both faced considerable personal danger.

---

[a]39 Greek *a hundred litrai* (about 34 kilograms)

¹⁵"Woman," he said, "why are you crying? Who is it you are looking for?"

Thinking he was the gardener, she said, "Sir, if you have carried him away, tell me where you have put him, and I will get him."

¹⁶Jesus said to her, "Mary."

She turned toward him and cried out in Aramaic, "Rabboni!" (which means Teacher).

¹⁷Jesus said, "Do not hold on to me, for I have not yet returned to the Father. Go instead to my brothers and tell them, 'I am returning to my Father and your Father, to my God and your God.'"

¹⁸Mary Magdalene went to the disciples with the news: "I have seen the Lord!" And she told them that he had said these things to her.

JESUS APPEARS TO HIS DISCIPLES

¹⁹On the evening of that first day of the week, when the disciples were together, with the doors locked for fear of the Jews, Jesus came and stood among them and said, "Peace be with you!" ²⁰After he said this, he showed them his hands and side. The disciples were overjoyed when they saw the Lord.

²¹Again Jesus said, "Peace be with you! As the Father has sent me, I am sending you." ²²And with that he breathed on them and said, "Receive the Holy Spirit. ²³If you forgive anyone his sins, they are forgiven; if you do not forgive them, they are not forgiven."

JESUS APPEARS TO THOMAS

²⁴Now Thomas (called Didymus), one of the Twelve, was not with the disciples when Jesus came. ²⁵So the other disciples told him, "We have seen the Lord!"

But he said to them, "Unless I see the nail marks in his hands and put my finger where the nails were, and put my hand into his side, I will not believe it."

²⁶A week later his disciples were in the house again, and Thomas was with them. Though the doors were locked, Jesus came and stood among them and said, "Peace be with you!" ²⁷Then he said to Thomas, "Put your finger here; see my hands. Reach out your hand and put it into my side. Stop doubting and believe."

²⁸Thomas said to him, "My Lord and my God!"

²⁹Then Jesus told him, "Because you have seen me, you have believed; blessed are those who have not seen and yet have believed."

³⁰Jesus did many other miraculous signs

WHO WAS "DOUBTING THOMAS"?

Thomas was one of Jesus' disciples who said he would not believe that Jesus had come back to life unless he could see Him in person and touch the nail marks in His hands and feet. Jesus granted Thomas his request, but then went on to say, "Blessed are those who have not seen and yet have believed" (20:29). That refers to anyone at the time or in future generations who believes without actually seeing Jesus in the flesh.

in the presence of his disciples, which are not recorded in this book. **31But these are written that you may**[a] **believe that Jesus is the Christ, the Son of God, and that by believing you may have life in his name.**

JESUS AND THE MIRACULOUS CATCH OF FISH

21 Afterward Jesus appeared again to his disciples, by the Sea of Tiberias.[b] It happened this way: 2Simon Peter, Thomas (called Didymus), Nathanael from Cana in Galilee, the sons of Zebedee, and two other disciples were together. 3"I'm going out to fish," Simon Peter told them, and they said, "We'll go with you." So they went out and got into the boat, but that night they caught nothing.

4Early in the morning, Jesus stood on the shore, but the disciples did not realize that it was Jesus.

5He called out to them, "Friends, haven't you any fish?"

"No," they answered.

6He said, "Throw your net on the right side of the boat and you will find some." When they did, they were unable to haul the net in because of the large number of fish.

7Then the disciple whom Jesus loved said to Peter, "It is the Lord!" As soon as Simon Peter heard him say, "It is the Lord," he wrapped his outer garment around him (for he had taken it off) and jumped into the

[a]31 Some manuscripts *may continue to*   [b]1 That is, Sea of Galilee

JOHN 20:31

That You May Believe

JOHN WROTE HIS Gospel to encourage belief in Jesus and establish His true identity as the Son of God. He explained, "These are written that you may believe that Jesus is the Christ, the Son of God, and that by believing you may have life in his name." Some of the sermons, teachings, and miracles recorded in the other three Gospels aren't in this book and some of what John records is unique to his Gospel. The other Gospels were already circulating throughout the early churches; John added a unique perspective by writing from his own personal experience with Jesus.

The last verse of John's Gospel is truly amazing. He says that Jesus did many other things that are not recorded in his book, and if they were written down the whole would not have room for the books that would be written. In other words, John has written just enough in his Gospel that you may believe, but there is even more that could have been recorded!

water. ⁸The other disciples followed in the boat, towing the net full of fish, for they were not far from shore, about a hundred yards.ᵃ ⁹When they landed, they saw a fire of burning coals there with fish on it, and some bread.

¹⁰Jesus said to them, "Bring some of the fish you have just caught."

¹¹Simon Peter climbed aboard and dragged the net ashore. It was full of large fish, 153, but even with so many the net was not torn. ¹²Jesus said to them, "Come and have breakfast." None of the disciples dared ask him, "Who are you?" They knew it was the Lord. ¹³Jesus came, took the bread and gave it to them, and did the same with the fish. ¹⁴This was now the third time Jesus appeared to his disciples after he was raised from the dead.

JESUS TELLS PETER TO FOLLOW HIM

¹⁵When they had finished eating, Jesus said to Simon Peter, "Simon son of John, do you truly love me more than these?"

"Yes, Lord," he said, "you know that I love you."

Jesus said, "Feed my lambs."

¹⁶Again Jesus said, "Simon son of John, do you truly love me?"

He answered, "Yes, Lord, you know that I love you."

Jesus said, "Take care of my sheep."

¹⁷The third time he said to him, "Simon son of John, do you love me?"

Peter was hurt because Jesus asked him the third time, "Do you love me?" He said, "Lord, you know all things; you know that I love you."

Jesus said, "Feed my sheep. ¹⁸I tell you the truth, when you were younger you dressed yourself and went where you wanted; but when you are old you will stretch out your hands, and someone else will dress you and lead you where you do not want to go." ¹⁹Jesus said this to indicate the kind of death by which Peter would glorify God. Then he said to him, "Follow me!"

²⁰Peter turned and saw that the disciple whom Jesus loved was following them. (This was the one who had leaned back against Jesus at the supper and had said, "Lord, who is going to betray you?") ²¹When Peter saw him, he asked, "Lord, what about him?"

²²Jesus answered, "If I want him to remain alive until I return, what is that to you? You must follow me." ²³Because of this, the rumor spread among the brothers that this disciple would not die. But Jesus did not say that he would not die; he only said, "If I want him to remain alive until I return, what is that to you?"

²⁴This is the disciple who testifies to these things and who wrote them down. We know that his testimony is true.

²⁵Jesus did many other things as well. If every one of them were written down, I suppose that even the whole world would not have room for the books that would be written.

ᵃ8 Greek *about two hundred cubits* (about 90 meters)

A STEP OF FAITH

THE NEW TESTAMENT makes it clear that we have to do something to accept the gift that God offers. John writes that "God so loved the world that he gave his one and only Son, that whoever believes in him shall not perish but have eternal life" (John 3:16).

BELIEVING INVOLVES AN act of faith, based on all that we know about Jesus. It is not blind faith. It is putting our trust in a Person. In some ways it is like the step of faith taken by a bride and a groom when they say, "I will" on their wedding day.

THE WAY PEOPLE take this step of faith varies enormously but below is one way in which you can take this step of faith right now. It can be summarized by three very simple words:

"Sorry"

YOU HAVE TO ask God to forgive you for all the things you have done wrong and turn from everything which you know is wrong in your life. This is what the Bible means by "repentance."

"Thank You"

YOU BELIEVE THAT Jesus died for you on the cross. You need to thank Him for dying for you and for the offer of His free gift of forgiveness, freedom, and His Spirit.

"Please"

GOD NEVER FORCES His way into our lives. It is up to you to invite Him to come and live within you by His Spirit.

IF YOU WOULD like to have a relationship with God and you are ready to say these three things, then here is a very simple prayer that you can pray to start that relationship:

> *Lord Jesus Christ, I am sorry for the things I have done wrong in my life [take a few moments to ask His forgiveness for anything particular that is on your conscience]. Please forgive me. I now turn from everything that I know is wrong. Thank You that You died on the cross for me so that I could be forgiven and set free. Thank You that You offer me forgiveness and the gift of Your Spirit. I now receive that gift. Please come into my life by Your Holy Spirit to be with me forever. Thank You, Lord Jesus. Amen.*

Further Reading

Books by Nicky Gumbel:

❶ ALPHA—QUESTIONS OF LIFE

The Alpha course in book form; looks in greater detail at the relevance of Jesus to our lives today.

❷ WHY JESUS?

A short presentation of Jesus, exploring common questions about His life and significance.

❸ 30 DAYS

Thirty passages from the Old and New Testaments that can be read over thirty days. Designed for anyone who is interested in beginning to explore the Bible.

❹ SEARCHING ISSUES

The seven most common questions raised on the Alpha course. Why does God allow suffering? Do all religions lead to God? Is there really a conflict between science and Christianity? Nicky Gumbel addresses these and other serious questions, often raised as objections to the Christian faith.

❺ A LIFE WORTH LIVING

How do we live life to the full? Based on the book of Philippians, this book is an invaluable next step for those who have just completed an Alpha course, and for those eager to put their faith on a firm biblical footing.

❻ CHALLENGING LIFESTYLE

An in-depth look at the Sermon on the Mount (Matthew 5—7) showing how Jesus' teaching flies in the face of modern lifestyle and presents us with a radical alternative.

❼ THE HEART OF REVIVAL

Ten studies based on Isaiah 40—66 drawing out important truths for today. This course seeks to understand what revival might mean and how we can prepare for it.

FINDING AN
ALPHA COURSE
NEAR YOU

IF YOU ARE interested in finding an Alpha course near you, please call or visit our Web site for more information. Resources can be ordered by phone, on the Web site, or in your local Christian bookstore.

OUTSIDE OF THE USA or Canada, please visit **www.alpha.org** to find your country information.

ALPHA U.S.A.
74 TRINITY PLACE
NEW YORK, NY 10006
TEL: 800 DO ALPHA
TEL: 800.362.5742
FAX: 212.406.7521
E-MAIL: INFO@ALPHAUSA.ORG
WWW.ALPHAUSA.ORG

ALPHA CANADA
11331 COPPERSMITH WAY, Suite #230
RIVERSIDE BUSINESS PARK
RICHMOND, BC V7A 5J9
TEL: 800.743.0899
TEL: 604.304.2082
FAX: 604.271.6124
E-MAIL: OFFICE@ALPHACANADA.ORG
WWW.ALPHACANADA.ORG

TO PURCHASE RESOURCES in Canada:
COOK COMMUNICATIONS MINISTRIES
P.O. BOX 98, 55 Woodslee Avenue
PARIS, ONT N3L 3E5
TEL: 800.263.2664
FAX: 800.461.8575
E-MAIL: CUSTSERV@COOK.CA
WWW.COOK.CA

NOTES

NOTES

NOTES

NOTES

NOTES

NOTES

NOTES